Orchids

Orchids

Liz Johnson

LONDON, NEW YORK, MUNICH, MELBOURNE, DELHI

PROJECT EDITOR Sarah Ruddick
PROJECT ART EDITOR Alison Shackleton
MANAGING EDITOR Esther Ripley
MANAGING ART EDITOR Alison Donovan
PICTURE RESEARCH Janet Johnson, Mel Watson
PRODUCTION EDITOR Kavita Varma
PRODUCTION CONTROLLER Danielle Smith
PHOTOGRAPHY Clive Nichols

US EDITOR Margaret Parrish
US CONSULTANT Delilah Smittle

First published in the United States in 2010 by
DK Publishing
375 Hudson Street
New York, New York 10014

10 11 12 13 14 10 9 8 7 6 5 4 3 2

[176602—March 2010]

Published in Great Britain by Dorling Kindersley Limited.

A catalog record for this book is available
from the Library of Congress.

ISBN 978-0-7566-5908-0

Printed and bound by Star Standard Pte. Ltd., Singapore

Important notice
The author and the publishers can accept no liability for
any harm, damage, or illness arising from the use or
misuse of the plants and processes described in this book.

Discover more at
www.dk.com

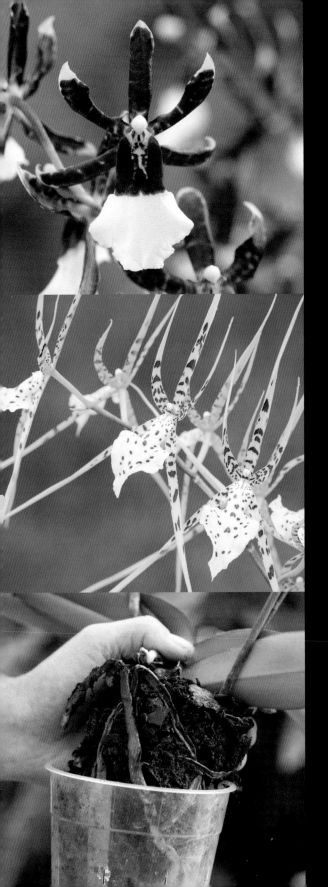

Contents

Liz Johnson is an RHS Orchid Committee
member, orchid judge, and an avid supporter of
orchid conservation. She is the owner of McBean's
Orchids, Sussex, England, a nursery founded in 1879,
which has a worldwide reputation for breeding and
exhibiting orchids, gaining countless awards.

All about orchids

Many plants have exotic flowers, but there is something very special about orchids. Whether it's their vivid colors, intricately painted faces, or pure elegance, there are orchids to suit all tastes. Some are suitable as houseplants, a few for growing outdoors, while others need more specialized conditions. Orchids are widely available from garden centers and flower shops, although you will find the best choice at specialized nurseries, which can also provide the best advice.

Past and present

From the collection of wild orchids to the production of artificially propagated plants, our fascination with orchids can be traced back 4,000 years to their use in Chinese medicine. Today, they are one of our favorite houseplants.

Pictures clockwise from right

Early beginnings A collection of pressed orchids was first created at the Royal Botanic Gardens, Kew, England, in the 18th century, but the passion for orchid collecting was not ignited until the 19th century, when William Cattley became the first person to succeed in actually flowering a plant. Collectors were sent out in pursuit of the new and fascinating. Huge consignments of orchids were ripped from the wild and sent back to England, although the vast majority perished before arriving. Records of the early collections can be found, not just in literature, but in the dedicated and exquisitely detailed recording of plants by botanical artists of the time *(see right)*.

Industrial revolution In the 20th century, new methods of germinating seed on agar in laboratories, followed by the discovery of cloning methods, made the mass production of plants possible. Orchids became much more affordable.

Silicon age Large-scale production of plants now takes place all over the world, with the majority of moth orchids now coming from Asia. The recent introduction of computer-controlled environments and modern factory equipment, such as conveyor belts and automated light, feeding, and watering systems, makes it possible for millions of plants to be produced with minimal human involvement. This has reduced the cost of plants considerably, making a basic range of inexpensive houseplant orchids available to all.

The future As a result of this industrialized approach, the amateur orchid grower is finding things more difficult, since small, specialized nurseries are now becoming more of a rarity. These nurseries cannot compete on price with the industrial giants, but it is here that you will find a wealth of advice and knowledge, as well as the more unusual orchids that appeal most to amateur growers and exhibitors.

Range of orchids

Orchids are arguably the largest family of flowering plants, with over 30,000 species and hundreds of thousands of registered and unregistered hybrids. Flower shape and size vary immensely, and orchids are found in almost every color, except true black. Although some are unperfumed, orchids have a range of scents—not all of them pleasant.

Pictures clockwise from left
Macodes petola comes from Sumatra and the Philippines, and is one of a group called jewel orchids. The flowers are insignificant; this orchid is grown for its attractive foliage. Its velvety green leaves are veined in gold, with the undersides a contrasting deep green, tinged with purple. When sunlight plays on them, they sparkle. Another jewel orchid, *Ludisia discolor,* is readily available and one of the easiest orchids to grow.

Vanilla planifolia is a native of Mexico and widely cultivated in the tropics as a source of vanilla pods, which are used in cooking and aromatherapy, and are also used to make perfume. The name comes from the Spanish *vainilla*, meaning "little pod." Pods on these orchids can grow up to 6 in (15 cm) long and contain precious vanilla seed, which is an expensive spice to buy.

Phalaenopsis pulcherrima syn. *Doritis pulcherrima* is found from northeast China to Borneo. Its dainty flowers, held on stiff stems, come in a range of remarkable colors, from pure white and white with a colored lip, to various shades of blue. This plant has been widely used for hybridizing to produce many of today's moth orchids.

Angraecum sesquipedale is often referred to as Darwin's orchid. On observing this orchid's exceptionally long spur and nocturnal scent, Darwin predicted that it must have a night-flying pollinator. Many years later, a hawk moth with an extremely long proboscis was discovered, proving Darwin right.

Range of orchids *continued*

Pictures clockwise from left

Dracula bella is a spectacular species from Colombia. Like many of the orchids in this recently established genus, it has an almost grotesque appearance. The name, from the Latin *dracula*, meaning "little dragon," also bears homage to Count Dracula from the famous Bram Stoker novel. Several species have been given "spooky" names, such as *Drac. chimera, Drac. diabola, Drac. gorgona,* and *Drac. vampire*.

Bulbophyllum falcatum, commonly called sickle-shaped leaf bulbophyllum, is an unusual species from Africa. A small plant, it produces a flattened rachis that resembles a knife blade, with tiny maroon flowers aligned horizontally on both surfaces. A magnifying lens is useful to see them.

Bulbophyllum Thai Spider is a man-made hybrid, producing an attractive mop of flowers on top of slender stems. These wave eerily in the breeze to attract insect pollinators. One of the parents of this hybrid is *Bulb. medusae*, which gets it name from Medusa in classical mythology—a monstrous Gorgon with wriggling serpents for hair.

Cypripedium x ventricosum is one of the slipper orchids, popularly called lady's or Venus's slipper as a result of their shape. Its modified lip or pouch is one of nature's great adaptations, forming a trap for any insect that is attracted to the flower. The only escape route for the insect involves climbing past the staminode, collecting or depositing pollen in the process, and ensuring fertilization.

Pleurothallis insigne is found throughout tropical America and is one of over a thousand species in a genus that runs the gamut of practically every orchid characteristic. They range from tall to short, single-flowered to multi-floral, with leaves thin to thick. These cool-, intermediate-, and warm-growing species have habitats ranging from wet to dry.

Hamelwellsara Happy Hour is the result of the hybridizers' constant quest to grow something new, or even bizarre, as a commercial houseplant. Recent breedings of *Hamelwellsara*, pioneered in Australia and New Zealand, have produced brightly colored flowers, in greens, purples, burgundy reds, and whites. This hybrid from the *Zygopetalum* alliance is made up of four different genera.

Range of orchids *continued*

Pictures clockwise from left

Psychopsis krameriana is always a show stopper. It is a member of a small but extremely flamboyant genus found from Costa Rica to Peru. Another very similar species is *Psychopsis papilio*. The genus gets its name from the Greek *psyche*, meaning "butterfly," and *opsis*, meaning "resembling." Indeed, there are several tropical butterflies that bear a close resemblance to these large flowers, which open slowly in succession, giving a long flowering season.

Stanhopea Hautlieu, like most plants in this genus, has an unusual growth habit—its strangely shaped flowers emerging from the bottom of the plant. Sometimes called the upside-down orchid, its short-lived flowers are spicily fragrant, not always pleasantly so. The plants are grown suspended in open wire or plastic baskets to allow the pendulous flower spikes to push through the base before opening. Spectacular to exhibit, these orchids are a nightmare for growers because their brief flowering period is difficult, if not impossible, to time precisely for an orchid show.

Vanda and its close relatives have long been admired, although it is considered something of a challenge to orchid growers in temperate climates. In its natural tropical environment, with high temperatures and high humidity, it is quite happy to grow suspended by wire, with little or nothing in the way of compost, and depending entirely on its aerial roots for moisture. There is currently a fashion for buying *Vanda* in clear glass vases. Although the plant can survive like this for several weeks, it is best to remove it after it flowers and hang it somewhere hot and humid. Frequent spraying is essential for the plant to reflower.

Coelogyne cristata, commonly known as string of pearls, has been a favorite of orchid growers for many years. Once abundant on trees in northern India, it was admired by the English botanist Sir Joseph Hooker, while plant hunting in the mid-19th century. This orchid produces drooping trusses of fragrant, frilly white flowers and creates a stunning effect when grown suspended in a slatted basket. Although a slow starter, the flower ball can reach 24 in (60 cm) or more in diameter and becomes extremely heavy.

Natural habitats

Most orchids grow in the tropics, but it is difficult to find an area of the world, from the Arctic Circle to Antarctica, that does not have its own native species. Many have specialized to grow in some of the world's toughest environments.

Pictures clockwise from left

***Dactylorhiza* are distributed** throughout Europe and the Mediterranean, the Himalayas, China, and Japan. North America and Madeira each have one species. They are Britain's most prolific orchid, inhabiting fields, marshland, golf courses, nature preserves, and private gardens, where they flower in June and July. They need a temperate climate and little competition to succeed.

Tropical cloud- and rainforests are home to most of the world's epiphytic orchids, where they cling to trees, sheltered by the leaf canopy. The low-level cloud cover of the cloud forests offers year-round moisture, while the high rainfall in the tropical rainforests sustains millions of plants. The good light, copious moisture, and high temperatures of these forests make an ideal home.

Orchids not only grow in habitats with vastly different temperatures, but they can also be found growing at greatly different elevations. Some of the reed *Epidendrum* grow high up in the Peruvian Andes in a very harsh climate. Clinging to the craggy rock, enveloped by passing clouds, and exposed to sun, wind, and rain, they blossom freely.

South African *Disa* plant their roots firmly in moist, free-draining soil, alongside streams, waterfalls, and wet cliffs, at 4,000 ft (1,200 m) above sea level. Known as The Pride of Table Mountain, *Disa uniflora* grows profusely on this sandstone substrate in open valleys and, more successfully, in rocky gorges.

The *Pterostylis* of Australia live in areas prone to summer bush fires. Most are winter-growing and die down to an underground tuber in the dry season, when the fires occur. The granite outcrops of scrub provide a harsh climate, and the rocky ridges, vulnerable to erosion and grazing by feral goats, provide an unlikely habitat.

Conserving orchids

The loss of orchid habitat caused by the clearing of tropical forests is well understood, but the destruction of important sites closer to home is often overlooked. The unauthorized collection and sale of orchids is also a concern.

To protect the world's wild populations, orchids are classified as endangered, and strict national and international rules control their trade. Orchids should never be taken from the wild to grow at home, since besides being an illegal practice, the transplants taken will seldom grow well. Instead, specialized nurseries have the techniques to grow and hybridize better orchids for the amateur. Buying nursery-raised stock also helps conserve wild plants.

Pictures clockwise from left
Cypripedium calceolus was once common in northern England; now, only a single plant remains. It is too late to save this orchid in England, but it survives elsewhere.
Masdevallia veichiana is shown here growing in Machu Picchu, Peru, at a sanctuary set up to preserve flora. Several countries have areas set aside to protect their native plant species.
Cypripedium acaule grows in many US states. It is currently classified as "endangered" in Illinois and "commercially exploited, endangered" in Tennessee.
Pleione formosana, and its forms, are widely available from nurseries, so there is no need for the illegal trade in plants collected from the wild.

Getting started

Very often, orchids are an impulse purchase, or received as a gift. Usually, this will be a moth orchid (*Phalaenopsis*), which is among the easiest to grow, but will often come with little or no growing advice, and will be thrown away after flowering. An unhealthy orchid or one that is unsuited to your home conditions is likely to fade quickly and bring disappointment. With tips on what to look for, where to buy, and how to find the right position for your orchid, this chapter will help you avoid potential pitfalls and choose the perfect plant for your home.

What is an orchid?

In spite of their enormous variety, orchid flowers share common characteristics. They are symmetrical but, unlike many blooms, can only be divided in half along one vertical plane, and all have a distinctive labellum or lip.

Flower structure Each orchid flower has three sepals and three petals, one of which is different in size, shape, and sometimes color. This distinctive petal is known as the labellum or lip. The male and female parts of the flower are fused together in a waxy column. This fusion is a key identification feature of the orchid family. Unlike most other flowers, orchids have pollen that is packaged into small masses called pollinia, which lie at the top of the column, under the anther cap; below the column is a stigmatic surface, usually sticky, to receive pollen. Each orchid seed pod can hold millions of dustlike seeds. These do not contain nourishment, so for the seed to develop, it must come into contact with a mycorrhizal fungus, which supplies the nutrition it needs.

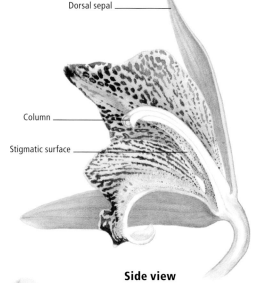

Dorsal sepal

Column

Stigmatic surface

Side view

Upper petal

Anther cap
This protects
the pollinia

Labellum
Large and colorful,
this often serves as
a landing platform
for pollinating
insects.

Lateral sepal

Cymbidium **flower structure**

How orchids grow

Orchids may be classified according to where they grow: in the ground, supported by other plants, or on rocks (*see below left*). They are also classified by how they grow, exhibiting one of two different growth habits.

Sympodial orchids, such as *Laelia* (*see pp. 96–97*), have a horizontal stem or rhizome system that produces new shoots successively. Often more than one growth is produced at a time, and the orchid is then described as having more than one lead.

Monopodial orchids have one main upright or pendant stem. Each year, growth occurs from the apex, which can be quite small, as in *Phalaenopsis* (*see pp. 120–121*), or much larger, as in *Vanda* (*see pp. 128–129*).

A sympodial orchid has several growing points.

A monopodial orchid grows from one point.

Epiphytes cling to other plants for support.

Terrestrial orchids grow on the ground with their roots in the earth. They get their water and nutrients from the soil, which is usually an open mixture of humus and leaf litter. *Paphiopedilum* (*see pp. 116–119*) and *Cymbidium* (*see pp. 82–85*) are both examples of terrestrial orchids.

Epiphytes grow on other plants, often trees. They are not parasitic and use the host plant purely for support. They obtain water and minerals through absorbent aerial roots. *Phalaenopsis* (*see pp. 120–121*) and *Vanda* (*see pp. 128–129*) are epiphytic orchids.

Lithophytes grow on rocks or in crevices. They get their nourishment from rainwater and thin layers of plant detritus or moss. The best known example is the rock orchid, *Dendrobium speciosum* (*see pp. 86–87*).

Buying orchids

It's always worth taking your time when choosing an orchid, since it is easy to be seduced by them. Check them over thoroughly for health, and make sure you know what conditions they require.

Where to buy

Reputable nurseries are the best places to purchase orchids; their experienced staff will be able to advise you. If buying over the Internet or by mail order, bear in mind that you will not be able to inspect the plant in advance, so choose your source carefully, and make sure that the orchid will be properly protected in transit. For a wide selection, consider going to an orchid show, usually held from late fall to early summer. Here, you will have the opportunity to compare and buy from a number of nurseries. Orchids are protected species, so be certain that the plants have not been taken from the wild when you buy. Import permits issued by the United States Department of Agriculture (USDA) are required for orchid purchases made outside North America.

You will be able to browse and choose from a wide selection of healthy orchids at a specialized nursery (*below*).

Choose the right type

First, consider the type of conditions you are able to offer an orchid: cool, intermediate, or warm (see pp. 28–29). Then decide whether you want a plant in bloom (some warm-growing orchids are available year round) or the satisfaction of raising a young specimen, bought from a nursery or online. *Phalaenopsis* (see pp. 120–121) is often a good orchid to start with if you have a centrally heated home and *Cymbidium* (see pp. 82–85) are some of the easiest cool-condition orchids. Always check the label to see what care the plant requires before buying. If the plant is unlabeled, seek advice from staff, or choose another specimen.

A healthy orchid like this *Oncidium* should have fresh flowers and green, pert buds. Reject any substandard plant.

Clear pots allow you to look for a healthy root system before buying a plant.

Health check

If you can see the orchid before you buy, inspect it carefully to make sure you're buying a healthy plant. Check for really fresh, blemish-free flowers (see above), with no drooping blooms or brown edges to the petals; any buds should be green and pert. Inspect the leaves, including their undersides, for any signs of pests and disease (see right and pp. 136–137). Reject any with shriveled leaves, which could be a sign of dehydration or root rot. If the growing pot is transparent, check for a healthy root system (above right). Unless you're buying an outdoor orchid (see pp. 60–71), reject any plant that is displayed outside.

The shriveled pseudobulbs on this *Cymbidium* indicate underwatering.

Yellow and brown patches on these leaves are signs of disease and insect damage.

Selecting and transporting

When you have chosen your plant, make sure it is wrapped well for the trip home, since orchids don't respond well to a cold shock. Before you buy an orchid online, check that you know exactly what is offered and how it will be delivered.

A healthy plant, like this *Burrageara* Nelly Isler, has clean, unblemished foliage and flowers, with no sign of shriveled buds. Given suitable care and conditions, it should continue flowering for weeks.

What size plant to buy It takes several years of growing before an orchid plant is mature enough to flower, but they can be bought from breeders at various stages of development. If you buy online, it can be difficult to understand the size of plants on offer, unless the site states clearly that the orchid is in bud or blooming. Here are a few terms used by nurserymen to describe the stages of growth:

• **Seed** Growing from seed is not recommended for amateurs.

• **In vitro** These plants are babies growing in sterilized jars on agar: a challenge for beginners to grow.

• **Ex vitro** These plants have been removed from their jars, and either planted singly or as a small group growing in a "community pot."

• **Young plant** Already several months or years old, this orchid may soon reach flowering size.

• **Near-flowering size** This plant may flower in the coming season but might need another year to mature fully.

• **Flowering size** This orchid is capable of producing a flower spike and may have already done so.

• **Mature** This plant has flowered for several seasons, although it may not be in bloom at the time of purchase. Check before buying.

Taking your orchid home

Make sure that any orchid is wrapped well for the journey. It will become distressed and is likely to drop its buds (*see pp. 136–137*) if exposed to cold or extreme temperatures. Wrap and unwrap carefully. As soon as you have the plant home, remove the transparent sleeve promptly to avoid any danger of grey mold, *Botrytis (see p. 135).*

Place the flower pot on a large sheet of tissue paper, which should be gathered up around the pot. This will help you get the plant into a sleeve.

Lower the plant into a transparent flower sleeve. Gently pull the sleeve up to protect the leaves. A longer sleeve protects the flowers, too.

Place the sleeved plant inside a box or bag lined with tissue paper. Pull the paper up around the top of the box, and gently over the flowers.

Positioning your orchid

Whether you have a single orchid or a small collection, finding the right spot for the plants in your home is essential. Be wary of drafty rooms or those with low light levels, and don't be tempted to place an orchid above a radiator.

Light is a basic requirement for plant growth. The majority of orchids are epiphytes (*see pp. 16–17*) and grow best in indirect sunlight that mimics the conditions they enjoy in the wild, such as the shade provided by their supporting tree. In your home, a windowsill with no direct sunlight, or a shelf close to a window, is ideal. To check the light level at your chosen spot, place your hand between your orchid and its light source, about 10 in (25 cm) away from the plant. If a shadow falls on the plant it is too near the light; either move it away or provide some shading, such as a sheer curtain. Be aware that the intensity of light changes throughout the year, and you may need to provide additional shading for your orchid in summer to help maintain a suitable temperature, as well as its preferred humidity level.

This mixed arrangement is happy in a warm living room.

An east- or west-facing windowsill is fine for a mixed collection.

A mantelpiece works for a temporary display.

This orchid sits away from the window, out of direct sunlight.

A cool, shaded sun room is often ideal for orchids.

A heated bathroom helps maintain humidity levels.

Temperature ranges should be as close as possible to those found in the orchid's natural habitat, and the simplest way to achieve this is to choose an orchid from a group that thrives in your home conditions (*refer to the directory on pp. 72–133 when selecting your orchid*). The following minimum temperatures are guidelines only; daytime temperature is the most important:

- Cool orchids: day 64°F (18°C), night 50°F (10°C)
- Intermediate orchids: day 68°F (20°C), night 55°F (13°C)
- Warm orchids: day 68°F (20°C), night 60°F (16°C)

Remember, rooms will be colder if the heating is off during the day, especially bathrooms, where tiles can be very cold. At night, don't trap your orchid behind curtains, away from its heat source and close to cold glass.

Humidity is essential for orchids, and the dry air commonly experienced in centrally heated houses can cause problems. The first symptoms are brown leaf tips or petal edges; some orchids drop their buds. Ensure that the room is well ventilated, and put your plant on a pebble tray (*see pp. 34–35*) to increase humidity.

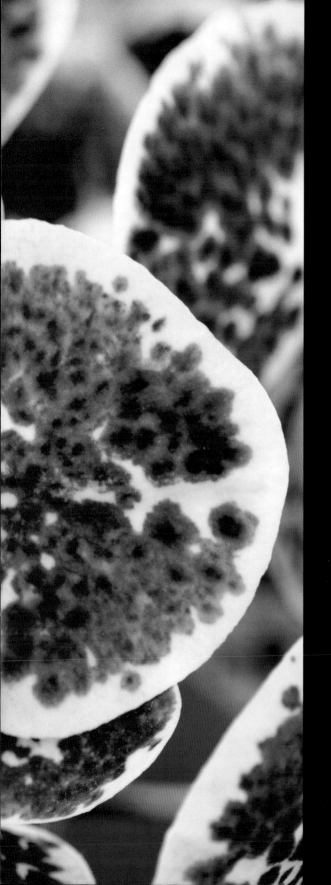

Looking after orchids

All orchids in cultivation require a suitable environment in which to grow, with adequate light, warmth, water, and food. Most plants sold for the home grower are no more demanding than other houseplants. Orchids such as *Phalaenopsis*, *Paphiopedilum*, *Cymbidium*, and *Oncidium* are among the easiest to grow and are ideal for the beginner; they will give great rewards once a few basic rules are mastered. Other genera can be more demanding, but the enthusiastic grower can succeed, given the right information. Tips on general care and tasks, such as repotting and dividing, are included in the following chapter.

Watering and feeding

Taking care of your orchids need not be time-consuming. Many are tolerant of neglect, but all orchids will respond well to good care. Follow this straightforward advice to help you water and feed your plants correctly.

Orchids absorb water from their growing medium; epiphytic orchids also take up moisture from the atmosphere via aerial roots. Most prefer water that is low in calcium; rainwater is ideal, but filtered or distilled water can be used (*see Fertilizers on opposite page*). Use water at room temperature to keep from shocking the plant.

To help judge when to water, weigh the pot in your hand when it is dry, then well watered. Most pot-grown orchids should be watered thoroughly from the top and allowed to drain—don't let the plant stand in excess water. Take care to keep the center of the plant dry to prevent rot. If water gathers between the leaves or in the crown, dab with some clean, twisted tissue to absorb.

Overwatering is the most common cause of death in orchid houseplants. Roots become "mushy" and unable to absorb moisture, and so the plant dehydrates and eventually dies. The commercial use of clear pots enables growers to check the health of the plant's roots.

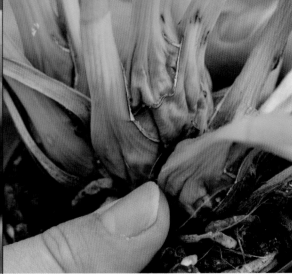

Underwatering symptoms vary from shriveled pseudobulbs (*above*) in *Cymbidium* and *Oncidium*, or floppy, wrinkled leaves in *Phalaenopsis*. Check the plant's roots to make sure that these signs of dehydration are not caused by overwatering before adjusting your regime.

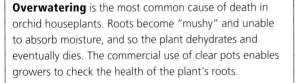

Leaves can be cleaned gently with a damp cloth when dusty or watermarked. Avoid the over-use of commercial sprays that make houseplants' leaves shine—too much product could affect the plant's ability to photosynthesize, causing serious problems.

Mist foliage gently in a dry atmosphere to increase humidity, but not at low temperatures or grey mold, *Botrytis (see p. 135)* may take hold. It is essential that epiphytes growing on a slab or suspended are misted, since this is the only way for them to absorb moisture.

Fertilizers

Most orchid compost contains very few nutrients. On the whole, orchids require very low levels of fertilizer, but the purer the water used, the more important a feeding regime becomes. Ordinary houseplant food is too potent for orchids as its chemicals can cause root burn. Be wary of ready-mixed orchid fertilizers; the amount of food required for different species can vary considerably, and one rate of dilution does not suit all. Use two specialty orchid fertilizers: a balanced one to help good plant growth during spring and summer; and one with a little more potash for fall and winter to encourage flower production. The changeover of food will coincide with the changing seasons and day length—this can come at any point in the orchid's growth cycle.

Overfeeding of orchids can cause problems: in the case of *Cymbidium*, too much nitrogen will cause plants to grow lush, strong green leaves instead of concentrating on flowering. If this happens, stop feeding for at least four months, and start again at the beginning of the fall/winter cycle. As with watering, the rule of thumb for feeding is: if in doubt, don't.

Liquid orchid fertilizer should be diluted according to the package instructions. For most orchids featured in this book, add the fertilizer when you water your orchid, but leave out the fertilizer every fourth watering to allow any residue to be washed through the compost.

Using a pebble tray

Create a microclimate for your orchid by using a pebble tray and a few small ferns. This easily maintained system helps to increase humidity levels and looks attractive.

Tip for success

Plants should be removed for watering. Top up the tray regularly, via the pebbles, making sure that the water level does not rise above the rim of the saucer.

1 Use a tray at least 1½ in (4 cm) deep. The choice of color and shape is yours, but the tray must be waterproof. Fill with clay pebbles—readily available from garden centers and most home stores—to within ⅓ in (1 cm) of the rim.

2 Place an upturned saucer on top of the pebbles and gently nestle it in, making sure that it remains above the level of the pebbles. Check that the saucer is large enough for your orchid pot to sit on comfortably.

3 Place the orchid pot on top of the saucer. The bottom of the pot must be high enough above the pebbles to keep the plant's roots out of direct contact with the water. The roots will soon rot if they become saturated.

4 Surround the orchid with ferns of your choice, standing their pots directly on the pebbles. These will help to regulate humidity levels. Most garden centers have a selection of small ferns at very reasonable prices.

Encouraging your orchid to reflower

Try this trick to help bring a *Phalaenopsis* back into flower. Alternate with cutting the stems down to 1 in (3 cm) to avoid exhausting the plants.

1 Just before the final flower dies, cut the flowering stem carefully with pruning shears or a clean knife, just above a node. Leave about 10–12 in (25–30 cm) of stem. Continue with routine watering and feeding.

2 Often, the node produces a secondary flower spike. If nothing appears after eight to 10 months, try reducing the plant's ambient temperature by 9°F (5°C) for four weeks. If the cut stem goes brown, remove it near the bottom.

Reflowering *Cymbidium*

Cymbidium orchids need good light and a significant lowering in night temperatures during the summer to initiate flower spikes for the following season. Ideally, the temperature differential must be about 14°F (8°C) for a couple of weeks, which is difficult to achieve in the home.

After any danger of frost is over, put the *Cymbidium* outside in a protected position with dappled shade. Gradually acclimatize it to more light. Watering depends on the weather, but make sure that the plant has good drainage. Placing the pot on a brick helps water to drain away and also deters slugs. Continue to feed the plant with a spring/summer fertilizer until the end of June. Stop feeding during July, starting again in August, using a fall/winter fertilizer; *Cymbidium* are not gross feeders and appreciate a break.

Bring the plant back indoors before the first frost and place it in a cool location. It is important to acclimatize *Cymbidium* gradually to an increase in temperature, since too abrupt a change will cause bud drop (*see p. 134*). To enjoy the flowers in the house as long as possible, wait until the blooms start to open before moving the plant.

Potting media and containers

Using the correct growing medium and container for a particular type of orchid is vital to the plant's health. The variety of pots and media can be daunting, but these tips will help you to choose.

Orchid potting media can be divided into two types: organic and inorganic. Organic materials include sphagnum moss, bark, and peat (*see opposite*), varying proportions of which are used as ingredients in potting mixes. Most inorganic media are based on absorbent rockwool. This material is not recommended for the home grower, since it can cause irritation to the skin and respiratory tract if not handled carefully. Mixing rockwool with organic materials should also be avoided.

Aerial roots, which are produced by all epiphytic orchids, absorb moisture from the atmosphere and should not be forced down into the potting medium. Any aerial root that has died off can be neatly removed without harming the plant.

A healthy orchid can usually be kept in the same container and growing medium for two to three years. When the roots fill the pot and the medium starts to break down (*see above and below*) it is time for repotting (*see pp. 40–41*).

Orchids can thrive in many different types of container, including plastic or clay pots, slatted hanging baskets, and on cork or tree fern rafts (*see pp. 42–43*). Whatever type of container you use, make sure it allows for good drainage. You can also place your plants in decorative pots (*see right*), but make sure that surplus water does not pool in the bottom of these.

Sphagnum moss mixes are used for seedlings, and orchids that like their roots to be cool and moist. This medium breaks down quickly and needs to be replaced annually. Water with rainwater or distilled water.

Orchid bark is the main ingredient of most mixes and is available in several grades, from fine to coarse. A medium or coarse mix provides good drainage and usually suits epiphytes. Some orchids will grow in unmixed bark.

An open mix of peat or peat substitute (coir fiber), medium bark, and perlite keeps most terrestrial orchids happy. The mix ensures good drainage, but also allows a certain amount of moisture to be retained.

Repotting

Spring is the best time for repotting an orchid, preferably when the plant is not in flower. Being repotted every two or three years suits most orchids, which benefit from a change of medium and the extra space for new growth.

1 The *Cymbidium* shown here has filled its pot with roots. To repot a healthy plant like this, support it with one hand and carefully knock it out of its pot. Strip away any old potting medium and trim back decayed or broken roots.

2 Select a new pot with good drainage that will allow space for no more than two years' growth. Compared with most plants, orchids grow well in pots that appear to be too small. Put a handful of potting medium into the pot.

3 Hold the plant in position and fill around it with more potting medium. Tap the pot lightly to work the mix through the roots. Lightly press the top of the medium and then fill the pot to within about 1 in (2 cm) of the rim.

4 Most potting mediums should be watered lightly and left for two weeks. If you are using sphagnum (*see p. 39*), water with rainwater thoroughly and allow to dry out completely before watering again. Do not give fertilizer for six weeks.

Repotting on a raft

Many epiphytes, particularly the small ones, take well to being planted on a raft, which is a piece of sterilized cork or bark. This allows the plants to grow in a natural-looking habitat.

Tip for success

When you tie your orchid onto the raft, use thin wires to fasten them. They can then be loosened easily if the plant needs to be given more room for growth.

1 To remove an orchid from an existing raft, carefully untwist or cut the wires that hold it in place. Gently tease out any spent sphagnum moss clinging to the roots and neaten up the plant by removing any dead material.

2 Either use a new raft or thoroughly clean the old one. You may find it easier to work if you place the raft on a support. Wet a piece of sphagnum moss with rainwater and apply it to the front of the raft.

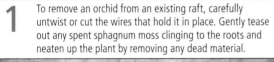

3 Mount the orchid on top of the sphagnum. The moss serves to hold moisture and stops the roots from drying out. Tie the orchid and moss to the raft with garden wire, making sure the plant is held firmly but not too tightly.

4 Lightly spray the finished raft with rainwater and then place it in your chosen growing position. You can either suspend the raft or use a stand. For dramatic effect, several rafts can be suspended together on a frame.

Propagation by division

Some orchids can be split
when they are large
enough, producing extra
plants to pass on to
friends. *Cymbidium* are
a good choice for division.

Tip for success

When you plant the divisions in pots,
the pseudobulbs should sit on the
surface of the medium. Water
thoroughly. Remember that new plants
usually miss the next flowering season.

1 Select a plant that has obviously outgrown its pot and cut the pot away with a sturdy knife, protecting your hands with gloves. Often, the roots completely fill the pot and there may be very little potting medium left.

2 Aim to produce divisions that each have three green pseudobulbs and one old brown one. Slice through the plant, trying to keep damage to a minimum. If you cut a bulb, remove it or dust it with approved fungicidal powder.

3 Examine the roots of each division to check on the general health of the plant. Gently pull out the remaining medium and strip away any damaged roots. Trim the rest of the roots to about 5 in (12 cm) in length.

4 New pots should be just big enough to allow for two years' growth. Repot (see pp. 40–41), positioning each division so that the old bulb is close to the rim of the pot, leaving room for growth from the green parts.

Propagation: other methods

Increasing your collection of orchids is never as straightforward as buying a package of seeds, but there are methods, other than division, that you can use to propagate certain types. However, many other orchids require specialized care and equipment to propagate successfully, which is best left to the experts.

Lab seedlings

When the Victorian plant hunters brought their new treasures home, they not only had to learn how to grow the plants, but also how to propagate them. Seed seemed the obvious method, but not all set seed naturally; many required hand-pollination as they lacked a suitable pollinator. Germinating the seed proved a great stumbling block, until it was found that mycorrhizal fungi needed to be present in the medium to establish seedlings.

An American botany professor, Lewis Knudson, was the first to show that orchid seed could be germinated in the laboratory on agar containing, not the fungi, but the sugars that the fungi provided naturally, plus some minerals. This was a great breakthrough. Today, millions of seeds are sown each year and are grown in controlled environments. A second major breakthrough was the discovery of the technique for cloning plants. Although not all orchids are easy to clone, most modern orchid houseplants are produced in this way.

Seed It is not unusual for an orchid to produce a seed pod. Natural pollination is usually the result of visiting insects, although orchids can also be pollinated by hand. Each pod contains thousands of seeds. The smallest seeds in the world are that of the *Ophrys*—they are like fine dust.

Lab In commercial laboratories, seed is sown in sterilized conditions onto special agar. It can take a year or more for the seed to germinate and, after moving on several times, grow large enough to be taken from their jars and planted. It is a highly specialized process.

Other methods of propagation

Topping tall plants Some orchids such as *Vanda* (*see pp. 128–129*) and *Vanilla* (*see pp. 10–11*) can grow rapidly, producing roots up their stems as they go and shedding their lower leaves. When it is actively growing, cut off the top of the plant, along with some aerial roots, and pot it. This will reinvigorate the original plant, and if the cut stem has any leaves and aerial roots left, it may produce more offsets that can also be removed and planted as well.

Keikis These are young plantlets that grow on the stems of epiphytic orchids (*see p. 23*). Wait until their roots are an inch long and cut through the main stem on each side of the keiki. Plant it in a tiny pot of damp moss. Water well with rainwater, drain, and place it in a warm propagator in a shaded position. Keep the plantlets at 68–75°F (20–24°C) by day, at least 64°F (18°C) at night, and keep the moss moist. After about three weeks, roots will develop, so feed with a very dilute orchid fertilizer. After three months, increase the food strength to normal. No ventilation is required for the first two weeks. After this, ventilate a little during the day to stop excessive buildup of moisture. Increase ventilation again after six weeks. After about six months, the keiki should be large enough to be repotted into fresh potting media. Handle it carefully.

Keikis are most common on *Dendrobium,* but can occur on any epiphytic orchid, including *Phalaenopsis.*

Propagate orchids from back bulbs

Remove bulb Use a knife to remove a hard, green back bulb (*see Glossary*), with a bud at its base, plus a small amount of root. Plant in a small pot of damp, fine bark medium and place in a shaded propagator. Mist and ventilate. After three months, a new shoot will develop.

Displaying orchids

Orchids can be a wonderful addition to almost any room in your home, but it's vital that you look beyond appearance and site your orchid in a place where it can flourish. For extra impact, you can buy ready-made arrangements in nurseries and flower shops, but creating your own is not difficult and is much more satisfying. This chapter takes you through a range of options to help you show your orchids at their best.

Table display

A simple table display is a great way to enjoy your orchids when they are in flower. The plants used here to striking effect are *Colmanara* Masai 'Red'.

1 Choose a plastic-lined basket that is deep enough to cover your plant pots with 2 in (5 cm) to spare. Fill the container with a layer of clay pebbles, or similar material, to allow for adequate drainage.

2 Water your plants thoroughly and let them drain before arranging them in the container. Make sure the flowers face the way you want. If necessary, adjust the clay pebbles so that the pots sit below the container's rim.

3 Carefully fill between and around the pots with more clay pebbles, up to, but not covering the pot rims. This gives easy access for frequent, but restrained, watering and helps to ensure that the pots do not sit in water.

4 Finish filling the container with moss or a decorative material of your choice. Colored wood chips and pebbles make an attractive finish and can be found at most garden centers. If you use moss, keep it sprayed lightly with rainwater.

Making an orchid corsage

You can easily turn a flower from an orchid, such as a *Phalaenopsis* or *Cymbidium*, into a beautiful wrist accessory for a special occasion.

Tip for success

If you own a glue gun, available from craft and hardware stores, use it for this project; the hot glue will ensure a firmer hold and a longer-lasting arrangement.

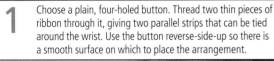

1 Choose a plain, four-holed button. Thread two thin pieces of ribbon through it, giving two parallel strips that can be tied around the wrist. Use the button reverse-side-up so there is a smooth surface on which to place the arrangement.

2 Pick two trimmed leaves, applying a leaf-shining product first, if you wish, and glue them on firmly to cover the button and provide a base for the orchid. Ivy is a good choice here; its structured leaves hold their shape well.

3 Pick as flawless an orchid flower as you can find, and cut its stem right back to the base so that it lies flat. Glue the flower on to the leaves, at an angle that will show it off at its finest when the corsage is tied on.

4 Allow the glue to dry, then use the strands of ribbon to tie the corsage firmly around the wrist. The orchid flower should stay fresh for the occasion and for a day or two afterward.

Orchid boutonniere

This eye-catching boutonniere is perfect for weddings or other special occasions. Choose long-lasting, structured foliage to complement the flower.

Tip for success

If you have time, wrapping the stems of your chosen foliage and orchid separately, before taping them together (*in step 3*), will make your arrangement even sturdier.

1 Cut an orchid flower with a short stem, then push florist's wire up into the back of the flower, through the stem. Push a finer piece of wire through the stem at right angles to the first. Loop it down on both sides and twist together.

2 Next, wire your chosen foliage. For eucalyptus, push the wire through the stem first, then loop around twice and twist the ends together. Known as "creating a leg," this process makes the foliage stronger and more flexible.

3 Arrange the foliage and orchid together, making sure that you're happy with your arrangement before wrapping florist's tape tightly around the stems. Take the tape down the stem, covering the end of the wire.

4 Decide on the length of stem you want to leave and trim the ends with sharp craft scissors. The boutonniere arrangement is now ready to be pinned onto clothing or attached with small magnets (available from craft stores).

Orchid bouquet

If your orchid plant is in full bloom, a bouquet of two stems combined with luscious foliage makes a beautiful gift that will last for two to three weeks, if kept in water.

Tip for success

Make sure you try out your arrangement before you finally tie it—think carefully about how foliage can be used to fill the gaps created by arching orchid stems (*above*).

1 Choose foliage that will complement your chosen orchid; if the flowering stems are long and arching, broad leaves, such as these *Fatsia*, will add balance. Spray with a leaf-shining product for a perfect finish.

2 If you've chosen to include long, narrow foliage, like these *Aspidistra* leaves, loop and staple after spraying for a structured, elegant look. Longer leaves will add height to the arrangement.

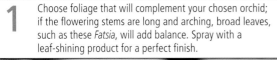

3 You can also use long grass stems to frame your orchids, folding them into loops and tying with thin strips of raffia to hold in place. The wider the variety of foliage you choose to include, the more lavish your bouquet will look.

4 Assemble your choice of foliage, together with the orchid stems, and tie together with ribbon or raffia, in a color that complements the flowers. You could then wrap the bouquet in tissue paper or colored cellophane.

Pole of orchids

This stunning pole display works best with orchids that have arching flower stems: try *Phalaenopsis* (*shown here*), *Oncidium*, or *Odontoglossum*.

1 Your pole could be a painted pipe or a thick bamboo cane. Find a safe spot and fix it securely: a Christmas tree stand is ideal. Use tape to attach empty plant pots to the pole; they should be the same size as those your plants are growing in.

2 Water your plants thoroughly and let them drain. Place them in the containers, turning them to face the right way for the desired effect. You could also use ferns or green trailing plants to enhance the display.

3 Wrap the pots in squares of floristry fabric or coconut fiber. Pull the fabric taut and neatly fold in any excess material. Secure with staples or straight pins, ensuring that no sharp points are left exposed.

4 To finish the arrangement, dress the tops of the pots with a small amount of greenery, such as Spanish moss (*shown here*). Place containers of ferns or other plants at the base of the pole to hide the stand and guard against knocks.

Outdoor orchids

Often overlooked, certain orchids are hardy enough to grow in the garden. Some are best suited to pots, but others can be planted out to form naturalized colonies.

Key to plant symbols

H	**Plant height**
	short: less than 8 in (20 cm)
	medium: 8–20 in (20–50 cm)
	tall: more than 20 in (50 cm)
F	**Flower size**
	small: less than 1 in (3 cm)
	medium: 1–3 in (3–8 cm)
	large: more than 3 in (8 cm)

Growing conditions

❄ ❄ ❄	fully hardy, grow outdoors all year
❄ ❄	grow outdoors; some frost protection
❄	needs frost-free greenhouse in winter

Soil preference

◌	well-drained soil
◐	moist soil
●	wet soil

Preference for sun and shade

☀	full sun
☼	light or dappled shade
○	full shade

Garden orchids

Once a rarity, outdoor orchids are being sold increasingly in garden centers and nurseries. Many can be grown outdoors in temperate climates, although some will fare better with winter protection in a frost-free greenhouse. By including some species in your garden, you will be helping to ensure their survival.

Dactylorhiza foliosa is hardy enough for cooler climates; if grown in a sheltered spot under suitable conditions, it can form large clumps with beautiful early summer flowers. It's ideal for "natural" gardens.

Orchids for shade Most garden orchids favor a bare patch of ground, where there is little competition from other plants, especially when they are young. The vast majority prefer light or dappled shade, and will grow happily beneath deciduous trees and shrubs, or in north-facing borders. Orchids suitable for shady conditions include:

- *Cypripedium calceolus (right), Cyp. flavum, Cyp. Gisela, Cyp. reginae (see pp. 64–65)*
- *Dactylorhiza fuchsii, Dact. maculata, Dact. praetermissa (see pp. 66–67)*
- *Epipactis gigantea (see pp. 68–69)*
- *Spiranthes cernua (see pp. 70–71)*

Orchids for damp areas, as well as shade, include:

- *Cypripedium flavum, Cyp. Gisela, Cyp. reginae*
- *Dactylorhiza praetermissa, Dact. purpurella*
- *Epipactis gigantea*
- *Spiranthes cernua*

Orchids for dry areas A few orchids enjoy a sunny spot and can be grown in a gravel garden. Try:

- *Anacamptis pyramidalis (see p. 64), such as:*
- *Ophrys apifera (see pp. 68–69)*
- *Serapias cordigera (below, see p. 70)*

Orchids for bright spots Most orchids dislike full sun but in a brighter spot, try growing:

- *Bletilla striata (left, see pp. 64–65)*

Orchids for containers Some orchids are best grown in containers in a frost-free greenhouse for the protection it offers when temperatures drop; these include the Mediterranean orchids that flower in spring. They can be moved indoors temporarily when in flower, then placed outside again for the summer. Orchids, such as *Serapias, Ophrys, Orchis,* and *Anacamptis,* are summer-dormant and should be planted in late summer, when they are just about to start their growing season. Orchids from cooler, more temperate climates, including *Bletilla, Cypripedium (top),* and *Dactylorhiza,* should be potted in late winter or early spring. Most terrestrial orchids with rhizomes are happy to be left in the same container for several years, while those with tubers (*see Glossary*) grow best when repotted annually. Always plant containers when the orchids are dormant.

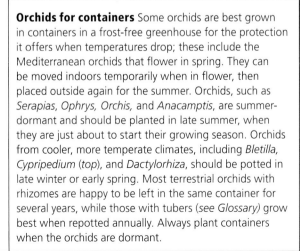

Orchids for the garden

Most orchids come from the tropics or subtropics, but some need only a limited degree of frost protection, while others are fully hardy. Many half-hardy orchids can be grown in a frost-free greenhouse. However, even hardy orchids need specific conditions if they are to thrive. This selection features plants that are available to buy raised from seed and not taken from the wild. Most are protected species (*see pp. 18–19*).

Anacamptis pyramidalis

Found from Europe to Northern Iran in poor chalk or limestone grassland. Can be grown in a sunny border or in pots, using a free-draining medium of equal parts sterilized loam, coarse grit, and leaf mold (preferably beech), with a dusting of dolomite lime. In the fall, a leaf rosette appears, followed by the flower spike in the following spring/early summer. Plants are dormant over the summer and require little watering. Tubers should be repotted each fall and watering gradually resumed, making sure that the potting medium dries out between watering. Hardy to 41°F (5°C); needs protection from frost.

H: medium; **F**: small
❋ ❋ ❋ ◊ ☼/☀

Cypripedium flavum

Species found in China. A white form is also available. Grow as for *Cyp. reginae* (*below*).

H: medium; **F**: large
❋ ❋ ❋ ◊ ☀

Cypripedium reginae

A native of North America, known as showy lady's slipper. Once established, can grow into a sizeable clump. Could be grown in pots or a raised bed, but looks best when naturalized in a cool, shady spot with plenty of moisture. Plant using a potting medium of equal parts sterilized loam, coarse grit, and sand. When growing in pots, never let the potting medium dry out completely, and refrain from watering when frost arrives. Dies down in fall; requires a cold period in winter to flower well the next year. Protect young growth from slugs and snails.

H: medium; **F**: large
❋ ❋ ❋ ◊ ☀

Cypripedium **Gisela**

A modern hybrid that has proved easier to establish and grow than *Cypripedium* species.

H: medium; **F**: large
❋ ❋ ❋ ◊ ☀

Bletilla striata

The Chinese ground orchid is known for its sweet fragrance. Found throughout China and Japan and is widely sold. Can be planted in a border in the fall or spring. Requires a rich, well-drained soil, and is happy in half-shade to full sun. In very cold areas, some winter protection may be required. A white form of this orchid is also available.

H: medium; **F**: large
❋ ❋ ❋ ◊ ☼/☀

Anacamptis pyramidalis

Cypripedium flavum

Cypripedium reginae

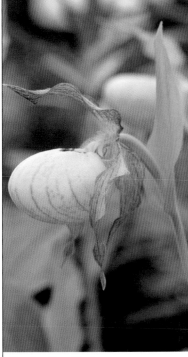

Cypripedium Gisela

Bletilla striata

Orchids for the garden *continued*

Dactylorhiza fuchsii

The common spotted orchid, so-called because it is the most common British native species, is found throughout Britain in calcareous or neutral grassland, without much competition from other vegetation. Flowers May–July. In common with other *Dactylorhiza*, it hybridizes freely. Hardy orchid, preferring cool temperatures and partial shade. Can be grown in most soils, ideally loam mixed with grit, sand, and leaf mold. Water freely when in growth. Plant while dormant, in early spring or fall; dies down after flowering in June/July.

H: medium; **F**: small
❀❀❀ ◊ ☀

Dactylorhiza praetermissa

The southern marsh orchid is probably the orchid species most suited to growing in the garden. Naturally found growing in large clumps in wet meadows or marshes, it must be kept moist. The inclusion of peat or a peat-free substitute to the growing mixture will help retain moisture. Dies down after flowering in June/July. Plant while dormant, in early spring or fall. Flower color may vary from pale pink to purple. Plants from western Europe usually have a flat lip.

H: medium; **F**: small
❀❀❀ ◐ ☀

Dactylorhiza maculata

The heath spotted orchid is found throughout Britain, in similar conditions to *Dact. fuchsii*, except that the soil is naturally acidic. It is more tolerant of shade.

H: medium; **F**: small
❀❀❀ ◊ ☀

Dactylorhiza purpurella

The northern marsh orchid is similar in most respects to its southern counterpart, but is not usually as tall. Grows in northern Britain, including the Scottish Isles, and is also found in Scandinavia.

H: medium; **F**: small
❀❀❀ ◐ ☀

Epipactis helleborine

In Europe, the broad-leaved helleborine is found in open spaces in forests, in undergrowth, and on roadsides. The species has been introduced into North America, where it has spread rapidly. Grows in most conditions but prefers calcareous soil, which should be kept moist while the plant is in growth. If growing in pots, allow sufficient room for the rhizomes to spread. Dies down after flowering in summer. Plant while dormant, in early spring or fall. Hardy to 41°F (5°C); may need some protection in winter.

H: medium; **F**: small
❀❀❀ ◊ ☼/☀

Dactylorhiza fuchsii

Dactylorhiza praetermissa

Dactylorhiza maculata

Dactylorhiza pupurella

Epipactis helleborine

Orchids for the garden *continued*

Epipactis gigantea
Native of North America. Thrives in moist conditions in the wild; often grows beside streams. Grows in partial shade or sun, in damp conditions or in a rock garden. Can spread to become a large clump; dies down after its summer flowering. Plant while dormant, in early spring or fall. Hardy to 41°F (5°C); may need some winter protection.

H: tall; **F**: medium
❄❄❄ ◊ ☼/☼

Habinara radiata
The egret orchid, from Japan and Korea. Best grown in containers that can be brought inside for winter, or in a cold frame. Keep cool and shaded at all times. In early spring, plant the pealike tubers into an open orchid potting medium containing peat or peat substitute to retain moisture. Water freely with rainwater from early spring to the end of the summer, keeping the medium wet but not stagnant. Will die down after flowering. Give a winter rest period, keeping the medium just damp. Repot when the first new growths appear.

H: medium; **F**: medium
❄❄❄ ◊ ☼

Ophrys apifera
The genus *Ophrys* consists mainly of Mediterranean plants, but *Oph. apifera*, the bee orchid, is also native to Britain. All *Ophrys* are protected species that should not be dug up. In cultivation, grow in pots in a cold frame; they do not like damp, cold conditions. Use free-draining potting medium of equal parts sterilized loam, coarse grit, and leaf mold (preferably beech), with a dusting of dolomite lime. Produces a leaf rosette in fall, and the flower spike in the following spring/early summer. After flowering, the plant will die down. Stop watering and rest the plant; resume watering in September. This species is almost always self-pollinating.

H: medium; **F**: medium
❄ ◊ ☼/☼

Ophrys lutea
The yellow bee orchid is found in coastal Mediterranean regions, in shrubby, mostly evergreen vegetation, often on slopes, and usually in full sun in calcareous soil. Grow as for *Oph. apifera*.

H: medium; **F**: medium
❄ ◊ ☼/☼

Ophrys scolopax
The woodcock orchid, widespread across coastal Mediterranean regions, grows in shrubby, mostly evergreen vegetation, usually in full sun in calcareous soil. Variable in patterning and shape. Grow as for *Oph. apifera*.

H: medium; **F**: medium
❄ ◊ ☼/☼

Epipactis gigantea

Habenaria radiata

hrys apifera   *Ophrys lutea*   *Ophrys scolopax*

Orchids for the garden *continued*

Serapias cordigera

The heart-lipped tongue orchid, found from the Mediterranean through to Turkey. Can be planted in a sheltered spot in the garden, but prefers a raised bed or pot. Will seed freely in good conditions, making large colonies. Grow in a free-draining potting medium of equal parts sterilized loam, coarse grit, and leaf mold (preferably beech), with a dusting of dolomite lime. Flowers in late spring/early summer. Requires frost protection.

H: medium; **F**: small
❄❄ ◊ ☼/☀

Orchis italica

Short-lived perennial Mediterranean species, found growing in pine forests and shrubby, mostly evergreen coastal vegetation, usually in full sun on calcareous soil. Can form a large colony. Grow in a frost-free cold frame to protect the young growth that appears over winter. Plant in a free-draining medium of equal parts sterilized loam, coarse grit, and leaf mold (preferably beech), and a dusting of dolomite lime. Protect young foliage from slugs and snails.

H: medium; **F**: small
❄ ◊ ☼/☀

Ophrys insectifera

The fly orchid, native to Europe and found in Britain. Although resembling a fly to attract a pollinator, pollination is usually carried out by bees when they attempt to mate with it, attracted by the flower's appearance and also by its scent, which mimics the sexual pheromones of a fly. Prefers an alkaline soil. Grow as for *Oph. apifera*, leaving out the dolomite lime in the potting medium.

H: medium; **F**: medium
❄ ◊ ☼/☀

Spiranthes cernua

The lady's tresses orchid is native to North America and grows by streams, and in wet meadows and damp woods. Can be planted in most open, moisture-retentive soils. In the fall, the fragrant, densely arranged flowers spiral around the stems. In contrast, the native British species, *Spiranthes spiralis*, Autumn Lady's Tresses, grows in dry conditions and has much smaller and weaker flower spikes.

H: medium; **F**: small
❄❄❄ ◊ ☼/☀

Ophrys speculum

The mirror orchid is named for its shiny, reflective lip. It is found growing around the Mediterranean on calcareous soil in full sun, often near populations of *Oph. lutea*. In common with all the *Ophrys* species, *Oph. speculum* is summer-dormant. As its rosette of new leaves gradually appears above ground, a new tuber forms below, and its old one slowly dies. Grow as for *Oph. apifera*.

H: medium; **F**: medium
❄ ◊ ☼/☀

Serapias cordigera

Orchis italica

Ophrys insectifera

Spiranthes cernua

Ophrys speculum

Indoor orchids directory

Key to plant symbols

H **Plant height**

short: less than 8 in (20 cm)

medium: 8–20 in (20–50 cm)

tall: more than 20 in (50 cm);

F **Flower size**

small: less than 1 in (3 cm)

medium: 1–3 in (3–8 cm)

large: more than 3 in (8 cm)

Watering

♦♦♦ Keep moist at all times

♦♦ Do not allow to dry out completely between watering

♦ Allow to dry out between watering

R Needs a rest period

Light preference

☀ Good indirect light

☀ Partial or dappled shade

Preferred growing temperatures

Minimum requirements

Warm: day 68°F (20°C); night 61°F (16°C)

Intermediate: day 68°F (20°C); night 55°F (13°C)

Cool: day 64°F (18°C); night 50°F (10°C)

Angraecum

This diverse group includes over 100 species of epiphytes, most of which are night-scented, with ivory or white flowers and leathery leaves. Grow *Angraecum* suspended in baskets or in pots with excellent drainage, in an airy position with high humidity. They resent disturbance, so repot in open, bark-based medium only when completely root-bound. When repotting, soak the stiff aerial roots in warm water for up to 10 minutes to keep them from snapping off.

Angraecum calceolus
Found on islands of the Indian Ocean and Mozambique. Can form a large clump of short stems, with branching spikes of widely spaced flowers.

H: short; **F**: large
◊ ◊ ☼ warm

Angraecum Veitchii
Robust hybrid of *Angcm. eburneum* and *Angcm. sesquipedale*, registered in 1899. Winter-flowering, each inflorescence carries up to 10 blooms with slender spurs of about 6 in (15 cm) long.

H: tall; **F**: large
◊ ◊ ☼ warm

Angraecum sesquipedale
Spicily night-scented Madagascan orchid (*see p. 10*). Small plants may be grown in pots. They can form dense clumps of more than 3 ft (1 m) in height. Five or six large flowers appear on each spike in late winter or spring, characterized by their long spur of more than 1 ft (30 cm).

H: tall; **F**: large
◊ ◊ ☼ warm

Angraecum eburneum
A popular species better suited to a heated greenhouse than the home; forms large, robust plants with thick roots. Produces long spikes of large, showy flowers; some varieties have spurs up to 14 in (36 cm) long.

H: tall; **F**: large
◊ ◊ ☼ warm

Angraecum calceolus   *Angraecum* Veitchii 'Tokyo'

Angraecum sesquipedale

Angraecum eburneum

Brassia

Known as the "spider orchid," *Brassia* is a group of over 30 species, mainly epiphytes. These plants need a medium-grade bark mix and plenty of room for their flower spikes to develop. Normally, only the lower half of the spike is staked to show off its arching habit. Repot *Brassia* every two or three years in spring when 2 in (5 cm) of new growth from the base can be seen. When the pseudobulbs (*see p. 22*) are complete, reduce the temperature and keep plants almost dry.

Brassia verrucosa

Fairly tolerant epiphyte that grows best in daytime temperatures of around 82°F (28°C), with good humidity, and nights not below 57°F (14°C).

H: medium; **F**: large
◊◊ R ☼ warm with cooler period

Brassidium **Kenneth Bivin**

Easy-to-manage American hybrid, resulting from the crossing of *Oncidium* and *Brassia*. Can be grown in a pot or on a raft.

H: medium; **F**: large
◊◊ R ☼ warm with cooler period

Brassada **Orange Delight**

Summer-flowering American hybrid that enjoys a west-facing window. Grows well in daytime temperatures of 68°F (20°C) or more, with nights not below 54°F (12°C).

H: short; **F**: medium
◊◊ R ☼ warm with cooler period

Brassia **Rex**

Robust American hybrid. Needs plenty of space to flower well. A sizeable plant with very large flowers.

H: tall; **F**: large
◊◊ R ☼ warm with cooler period

Brassia **Arania Verde**

Scented American hybrid with two sizeable parents; will eventually produce a large, multi-spiked plant. Chosen for clearly defined spotting on large flowers.

H: medium; **F**: large
◊◊ R ☼ warm with cooler period

Brassia verrucosa

Brassidium Kenneth Bivan

Brassada Orange Delight

Brassia Rex

Brassia Arania Verde

Cattleya

This group of epiphytes and lithophytes can be grown indoors, given good light levels, humidity, and airflow. A temperature differential of 68°F (20°C) or more during the day, and 55°F (13°C) or more at night, is key to flowering. Water should be at room temperature. Repot mature plants in medium-coarse bark every two to three years. Plants can be divided (*see p. 44*) when large enough.

Cattleya intermedia
Produces three or more long-lasting flowers on each spike. Benefits from a winter drying-out period of three months; water every six weeks during this time, increasing the frequency in spring.

H: medium; **F**: large
◊ ◊ R ☼ intermediate

Guarianthe aurantiaca
Can make a very sturdy plant; each short flower spike carries up to 15 flowers that last for around one week.

H: medium; **F**: medium
◊ ☼ intermediate

Guarianthe skinneri
The national flower of Costa Rica; blooms in spring, producing up to seven purple flowers on a short spike. A white form also exists.

H: medium; **F**: medium
◊ ☼ intermediate

Cattleya bicolor
Subtly fragranced, grows well suspended in a well-ventilated but humid part of an intermediate greenhouse; produces spikes of up to 5 flowers in late summer. Likes slightly cooler conditions.

H: medium; **F**: large
◊ ☼ intermediate

Guarianthe bowringiana
Naturally lithophytic orchid, once widely cultivated; found in a range of colors, from mauve through deep pink to white.

H: medium; **F**: medium
◊ ☼ intermediate

Cattleya intermedia

Guarianthe aurantiaca

Guarianthe skinneri

Cattleya bicolor

Guarianthe bowringiana

Cattleya *continued*

Since its discovery, *Cattleya* have become great favorites with collectors and the public, for their showy, often fragrant blooms that are popular in corsages and bouquets. To increase the size and color range of plants and flowers available, hybridizers have crossed a variety of *Cattleya* with other genera.

Rhyncholaeliocattleya Paillette de Valec

Established French intergeneric hybrid with a slim tubular lip. More tolerant than a *Cattleya*, but still requires humid conditions. Expect two blooms per spike.

H: medium; **F**: large
◊ ☼ intermediate

Cattleya Aloha Case

Fragrant miniature *Cattleya* with two or three large flowers per spike. Blooms last up to three weeks; can reflower within the year. Good as a potted plant.

H: short; **F**: large
◊ ☼ intermediate

Cattleya Record

Established French hybrid with very distinctive "flaring" at the bottom of the lip. Take care not to spray the showy flowers, or they will mark.

H: medium; **F**: large
◊ ☼ intermediate

Rhyncholaeliocattleya Pralin de Valec

Modern French intergeneric hybrid with graceful, slightly dropping flowers. Usually produces two blooms per spike in early summer.

H: medium; **F**: large
◊ ☼ intermediate

Rhyncholaeliocattleya Love Call

Compact grower that produces large, rounded flowers. Colors vary from pale yellow through to orange.

H: medium; **F**: large
◊ ☼ intermediate

Rhyncholaeliocattleya Paillette de Valec

Cattleya Aloha Case

Rhyncholaeliocattleya Love Call

...*tleya* Record

Rhyncholaeliocattleya Pralin de Valec

Cymbidium (cool)

Once the most popular orchid genus, and one of the easiest to grow in a cool environment. *Cymbidium* prefer daytime temperatures of around 61°F (16°C) with nights down to 50°F (10°C); they can tolerate a wider temperature range, but will not flower as well. Grow in free-draining potting medium, and repot every two to three years after flowering, only when the pot is completely full of roots (*see pp. 38–41*). Water thoroughly when the medium is almost dry, and allow to drain. In a dry atmosphere, placing the pot on a moist pebble tray (*see pp. 34–35*) will help to prevent browning of the leaf tips.

Cymbidium **Ultimate Love**
American hybrid, "standard" *Cymbidium*; can make a substantial plant. Flowering in early spring, each spike can carry more than 10 long-lasting blooms. Young plants may have fewer flowers per stem.

H: tall; **F**: large
◊ ◊ ☼   cool

Cymbidium *tracyanum*
Found in China, Burma, and Thailand. During winter, produces large, slightly scented, spidery-shaped blooms on arching stems. Makes a large plant.

H: tall; **F**: large
◊ ◊ ☼   cool

Cymbidium **Sarah Jean 'Ice Cascade'**
Australian hybrid producing arching sprays of lightly perfumed white flowers in late winter/early spring. Can be displayed in a hanging basket.

H: medium; **F**: medium
◊ ◊ ☼   cool

Cymbidium **Strathbraan**
A McBean's-bred "miniature" *Cymbidium* hybrid, on average 18 in (45 cm) tall and with 3 in (7 cm), long-lasting flowers in late winter.

H: medium; **F**: medium
◊ ◊ ☼   cool

Cymbidium Ultimate Love

Cymbidium tracyanum

Cymbidium Sarah Jean 'Ice Cascade'

Cymbidium Strathbraan

Cymbidium (intermediate/warm)

These *Cymbidium* do not require substantial outdoor temperature differentials to flower well. Although a slightly cooler position for six to eight weeks after flowering would be beneficial, it is not crucial. The flowers of these *Cymbidium* are not as long-lasting as those of the cool-growing types. Intermediate- or warm-growing *Cymbidium* should not be placed outside if there is any danger of frost.

Cymbidium Golden Elf
A popular American hybrid, strongly scented and summer flowering. Each spike carries approximately seven clear yellow blooms.

H: medium; **F**: large
◊ ◊ ☼ intermediate

Cymbidium longifolium
Found from the Himalayas to the south coast of China. Forms large plants that produce lightly scented, elegant, close-set flowers on long spikes. Prefers a medium bark and perlite potting medium, which should be allowed to dry out between waterings.

H: medium; **F**: medium
◊ ◊ ☼ intermediate

Cymbidium dayanum
Occurring from northern India to China, and Japan to Sabah, in north Malaysia. Produces arching, pendulous flower spikes. Can be grown in a pot or hanging basket. Prefers a warm, humid atmosphere, a free-draining medium, and frequent watering all year round.

H: tall; **F**: medium
◊ ◊ ☼ warm

Cymbidium kanran
Originates in Southern China and South Japan. The Japanese name *kanran* means "cold orchid." Produces spicily scented blooms in winter/early spring. Allow to dry out between waterings.

H: medium; **F**: medium
◊ ◊ ☼ intermediate

Cymbidium Golden Elf

Cymbidium longifolium

Cymbidium dayanum

Cymbidium kanran

Dendrobium (cool/intermediate)

A variable genus of over 1,000 species, requiring a wide range of cultural conditions. Many cool- and intermediate-growing *Dendrobium* benefit from a cool, dry resting period in the winter to encourage flowering later in the year.

Dendrobium farmeri

Grow in a basket or on a raft to display its pendulous spike. Let medium dry between waterings. Enjoys an airy situation and shady conditions, with high humidity when in growth. Give an eight-week rest period at 46°F (8°C) for pale lilac or white flowers in spring.

H: medium; **F**: medium
◊ R ☼ intermediate

Dendrobium cuthbertsonii

Small species, just right for a cool window sill. Flowers are available in a wide range of colors, but are generally red.

H: short; **F**: small
◊ ☼ cool

Dendrobium densiflorum

Produces spikes of bright yellow, fragrant flowers in spring. Enjoys an airy situation and shady conditions, with high humidity when in growth. Let the medium dry out between waterings. Needs an eight-week rest period at 46°F (8°C).

H: medium; **F**: medium
◊ R ☼ intermediate

Dendrobium kingianum

Naturally lithophytic; a variable, tolerant species. Often produces keikis (*see p. 47*). A cool, dry, four-week rest period encourages flowering. Water freely when in growth, and repot every two years.

H: medium; **F**: small
◊ R ☼ cool/intermediate

Dendrobium Gatton Sunray

Classic, fragrant hybrid. Requires a four-week winter rest, free of water and fertilizer, to encourage flowering.

H: medium; **F**: medium
◊ R ☼ intermediate

Dendrobium cuthbertsonii

Dendrobium farmeri

Dendrobium densiflorum

Dendrobium kingianium

Dendrobium Gatton Sunray

Dendrobium (warm)

Many of the warmer-growing *Dendrobium* hybrids have been produced to provide cut flowers for the world's flower markets; these are often known as Singapore orchids or "Phalaenopsis types." Thailand is famous for its cut-flower orchid production, sending thousands of stems around the world each day. In ideal, warm and humid conditions, with bright, filtered light, these plants can grow all year round. *Den. biggibum* hybrids can make excellent houseplants.

Dendrobium **Anna Green**

Den. biggibum hybrid; needs bright, filtered light all year round, high temperatures, and medium/high humidity. Grow in a small pot of free-draining coarse to medium bark mix or pure bark. Requires staking to stabilize the plant. Repot every two to three years in spring, when 2 in (5 cm) of new growth is visible at the base. Water well when in growth, reducing frequency in the fall and winter. Mist gently in the morning if atmosphere is dry.

H: medium; **F**: medium
◊ R ☼ warm

Dendrobium **Thongchai Gold**

Den. biggibum hybrid. Grow as *Den.* Anna Green and *Den.* Burana White.

H: medium; **F**: medium
◊ R ☼ warm

Dendrobium **Burana White**

Another *Den. biggibum* hybrid. Grow as *Den.* Anna Green and *Den.* Thongchai Gold. Often used as a cut flower.

H: medium; **F**: medium
◊ R ☼ warm

Dendrobium **Sweet Dawn**

American hybrid that can be grown alongside the hybrids *Den.* Anna Green and *Den.* Burana White. Its different flower shape adds to its attraction.

H: medium; **F**: medium
◊ R ☼ warm

Dendrobium Anna Green   *Dendrobium* Thongchai Gold

Dendrobium Burana White

Dendrobium Sweet Dawn

Disa

The members of this showy genus are difficult to grow as part of a mixed orchid collection, but if their strict requirements are met, they are very rewarding. Pot-grow in either: live sphagnum moss; a mix of coarse peat and super-coarse perlite; or pure coarse sand. Sit in trays of rainwater or distilled water (changed regularly) when in growth, and water the pots from above with pure rainwater. Never allow the plants to dry out. *Disa* are intolerant of salt buildup, so feed with extreme care: a very weak solution of balanced orchid fertilizer can be added to the trays once a month during the growing season. Keep plants cool and protect from frost with a row cover in a heated greenhouse during the winter, when temperatures of 36–46°F (2–8°C) should be maintained. Repot in the spring every two to three years; plants can be divided at this time, when large enough.

Disa uniflora 'Red River'   *Disa* Kewensis 'Ann'

Disa uniflora
Produces one or two showy, fragrant flowers on each spike in spring and summer. Slower to bulk up than the other *Disa* species.

H: medium; **F**: medium
◊ ◊ ◊ ☼   cool

Disa Kewensis
Flowers in a large color range of pinks, lavenders, yellows, and oranges. Blooms are half the size of those of *Disa uniflora*.

H: medium; **F**: medium
◊ ◊ ◊ ☼   cool

Disa aurata
This species is distinguished by bright golden, slender, small flowers.

H: medium; **F**: small
◊ ◊ ◊ ☼   cool

Disa Watsonii
One of the first *Disa uniflora* hybrids, it is constantly being rebred by hybridizers.

H: medium; **F**: medium
◊ ◊ ◊ ☼   cool

Disa aurata

Disa Watsonii 'Sandra'

Doritaenopsis

Related to *Phalaenopsis* and also commonly called the "moth orchid", *Doritaenopsis* is easy to grow and makes an excellent houseplant. Naturally epiphytic, it is usually pot-grown in a very open medium containing bark. Modern hybrids are bred to produce two spikes with seven or more long-lasting flowers. *Doritaenopsis* can flower any time of the year, and may reflower within the year. It tolerates high temperatures as long as humidity is correspondingly increased. Water thoroughly when the medium is almost dry, and drain well. When in growth, water can be absorbed by the aerial roots. It does not require a resting period. Repot in alternate years in the spring, when not in flower.

Doritaenopsis Sin-Yuan Golden Beauty
Modern hybrid, popular for its unusual apricot coloring, which gives a very distinctive "warm" appearance.

H: medium; **F**: medium
◊ ◊ ☼ warm

Doritaenopsis White Wonder
American hybrid, one of the classic whites, popular for wedding and floral decoration. Many similar hybrids are available.

H: medium; **F**: medium
◊ ◊ ☼ warm

Doritaenopsis Ever Spring Prince
Taiwanese hybrid that produces amazingly patterned flowers. One parent is Golden Peoker, so patterns can vary, not only from year to year, but even from spike to spike.

H: medium; **F**: medium
◊ ◊ ☼ warm

Doritaenopsis Taida Sweet Berry
Striped Taiwanese hybrid, with a deep strawberry-pink web over a white base.

H: medium; **F**: medium
◊ ◊ ☼ warm

Doritaenopsis Sin-Yuan Golden Beauty   *Doritaenopsis* White Wonder

Doritaenopsis Ever Spring Prince

Doritaenopsis Taida Sweet Berry

Epidendrum

This large and varied genus is found throughout the tropical Americas. The name comes from the Greek *epi,* meaning "upon," and *dendron,* meaning "tree," which refers to the epiphytic growth habit of most of the species. Their culture varies, but most can be grown in intermediate conditions in an open orchid potting mix containing medium bark.

Epidendrum ibaguense
Lithophytic or terrestrial species found from Mexico to Argentina. Produces many brilliantly colored flowers that form a ball at the end of the flower spike. Prefers open orchid mix and unvarying conditions.

H: medium; **F**: small
◊ ◊ ☼   intermediate/warm

Epidendrum pseudepidendrum
Rare species found in Costa Rica and Panama. Cane-type plant. Requires high humidity and copious watering when in growth, and a semi-dry winter rest. Brilliantly colored flowers with a "plastic" gloss for protection against hummingbirds. Has been commercially propagated to safeguard the remaining wild specimens.

H: tall; **F**: medium
◊ ◊ R ☼   intermediate/warm

Epidendrum stamfordianum
Found in dry lowlands in Mexico, Panama, Venezuela, and Colombia. Water well when in growth. After flowering, requires a brief, dry rest period with increased light. Produces masses of fragrant flowers on arching stems.

H: tall; **F**: medium
◊ ◊ R ☼   warm

Epidendrum ibaguense x radicans
Hybrid of two popular species. Produces a brilliantly colored ball of small flowers. Grow in a pot of very open, bark-based medium. Does not require a rest period; enjoys humidity and frequent watering.

H: tall; **F**: small
◊ ◊ ☼   intermediate

Epidendrum ibaguense

Epidendrum pseudepidendrum

Epidendrum stamfordianum

Epidendrum ibaguense x *radicans*

Laelia

Found in Mexico, Central America, the West Indies, and across Brazil, *Laelia* bears a close resemblance to *Cattleya* and *Prosthechea*. Grow in a very free-draining potting medium in pots or hanging baskets, or suspended on a raft (see p. 42). Most *Laelia* require high light levels and a dry rest period.

Laelia anceps
The classic corsage orchid, with fragrant, showy blooms produced on tall flower stems. Water freely while growing but allow the roots to dry out between waterings. Needs a cool, dry rest period in winter.

H: tall; **F**: large
◊ R ☼ cool/intermediate

Laelia speciosa
Semi-dwarf Mexican species, grown in small pots or baskets, in a slightly denser medium than other *Laelia*. Requires a dry rest period with infrequent watering—just enough to stop the pseudobulbs form shriveling.

H: short; **F**: large
◊ R ☼ intermediate

Laelia gouldiana
Mexican species with tall flower stems. May require staking with a plant stake or two to keep it stable, particularly when mature. Grow as for *L. anceps*.

H: tall; **F**: large
◊ R ☼ intermediate

Laelia anceps

Laelia speciosa

Laelia gouldiana

Lycaste

This genus of epiphytic and lithophytic orchids comes from Latin America. The yellow-flowered plants lose their leaves at the end of the growing season, but the rest keep them for 18 months. Most can be grown at a winter night minimum of 54°F (12°C) and a day temperature of around 64°F (18°C), and at temperatures up to 86°F (30°C), with high humidity and good air movement during their growth period. Use a free-draining orchid medium and provide light shade when temperatures rise above 59°F (15°C). Some *Lycaste* have large leaves that make them unsuitable for growing in the house. Water freely while the new leaves and bulbs grow; keep drier during winter rest.

Lycaste skinneri
Showy flower color can vary from white to pink, often with a spotted lip. Makes a good houseplant when grown in cool, humid shade with excellent drainage.

H: tall; **F**: large
◊◊ R ☀ cool

Lycaste aromatica
Epiphytic or lithophytic, found in the higher altitude cloud forests of Mexico, Guatemala, and Nicaragua. Produces up to 15 cinnamon-scented flowers from the base of each pseudobulb.

H: medium; **F**: medium
◊◊ R ☀ intermediate

Lycaste dowiana
Flowers sequentially in summer. Needs excellent drainage and some water when at rest. Large plants can be divided after flowering into pieces with three back bulbs (*see p. 47*) and a vigorous lead bulb.

H: medium; **F**: medium
◊◊ R ☀ intermediate

Lycaste deppei
Easy-to-grow species. Flowers best after a long, dry rest period. Produces up to 10 blooms from the base of each pseudobulb.

H: medium; **F**: medium
◊◊ R ☀ intermediate

Lycaste skinneri

Lycaste aromatica

Lycaste dowiana

Lycaste deppei

Masdevallia

These cool-growing epiphytes are mostly found in the Andes, and the majority have tricorn-shaped flowers with "tails" on the sepals. Their natural growing conditions are cool, airy, yet humid, which is a challenging balance to achieve in the home; hybrids have been bred to be less demanding. *Masdevallia* can be grown in a sphagnum moss mix, which should not be allowed to dry out completely. Plants should be repotted annually.

Masdevallia yungasensis
Found in the Bolivian cloud forests. Grow in partial shade in small pots of fine bark mixed with perlite. Keep cool at all times. Produces a single candy-striped flower on each spike in winter.

H: short; **F**: medium
◊ ◊ ☼ cool

Masdevallia Shuttryana
Hybrid (*Masd. coccinea* x *caudata*), first registered by English orchid enthusiast Sir Trevor Lawrence in 1892. Produces many relatively large, brilliantly colored flowers with long tails. A small plant.

H: short; **F**: medium
◊ ◊ ☼ cool

Masdevallia coccinea
Cold terrestrial orchid found by rocky cliffs in Colombia and Peru. In spring, produces single flowers held above the leaves; most are deep magenta to crimson, but pale yellow/white forms have been found.

H: medium; **F**: medium
◊ ◊ ☼ cool

Masdevallia schlimii
From Colombia and Venezuela, and likes cold conditions. Produces four to eight two-toned flowers per spike, held well above the leaves, in spring/early summer.

H: medium; **F**: small
◊ ◊ ☼ cool

Masdevallia yungasensis

Masdevallia Shuttryana 'Lucy'

asdevallia coccinea

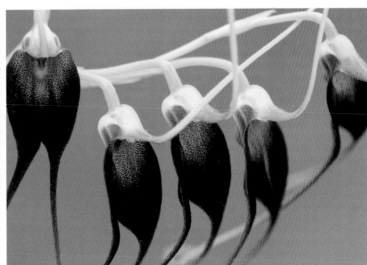

Masdevallia schlimii 'Eva May'

Miltonia

All *Miltonia* are found in South America, mainly in Brazil. They were named in honor of Viscount Fitzwilliam Milton, but are commonly called "pansy orchids." Grow in a medium bark mix, which should not be allowed to dry out; avoid fluctuations in watering and humidity, since these can cause a corrugated effect on the leaves. In a dry atmosphere, mist the leaves in the morning, or use a pebble tray (*see pp. 34–35*).

Miltonia flavescens
Requires a greater day/night temperature differential than other *Miltonia*. Produces fragrant, star-shaped flowers in summer.

H: short; **F**: medium
◊ ◊ ☼ intermediate

Miltonia spectabilis
The common form of this species, from the Brazilian rainforest, is pale yellow with a white lip. The deep plum variation *Milt. spectabilis* var. *moreliana* is most often found in cultivation.

H: short; **F**: medium
◊ ◊ ☼ intermediate

Miltonia Sunset
An American hybrid, with *Milt. regnelli* as one of its parents. Bred to produce long spikes of well-spaced flowers that thrive in high humidity.

H: short; **F**: medium
◊ ◊ ☼ intermediate

Miltonia clowesii
From southeastern Brazil. Produces long spikes of seven of more flowers, which open successively. Grow in good light and water evenly all year round.

H: medium; **F**: medium
◊ ◊ ☼ intermediate

Miltonia flavescens

Miltonia spectabilis var. *moreliana*

Miltonia Sunset

Miltonia clowesii

Miltoniopsis

A genus of six species, found across South America, from which most of the commercial pansy orchids have been bred. *Miltoniopsis* prefers to be grown below 68°F (20°C), with nighttime temperatures around 57°F (14°C), in open medium that should not be allowed to dry out. Water freely when in growth, reducing the frequency as temperatures fall. Although happy in partial shade, dark foliage is a sign of insufficient light.

Miltoniopsis **Newton Falls**
American hybrid, producing spikes of long-lasting, scented flowers during spring and early summer. Known as a "waterfall type" because of its lip markings.

H: short; **F**: medium
◊ ◊ ☀ intermediate

Miltoniopsis **Jean Carlson**
Fragrant American hybrid with solid coloring and a contrasting disk on the lip. Aerial roots are sometimes seen outside the pot of this and all *Miltoniopsis*.

H: short; **F**: medium
◊ ◊ ☀ intermediate

Miltoniopsis **Andy Easton**
American hybrid with white base and delicate coloring, intensifying toward the flower' center. As with all *Miltoniopsis*, repot soon after the flowers die.

H: short; **F**: medium
◊ ◊ ☀ intermediate

Miltoniopsis **Hajime Ono**
Striking "waterfall lip"; a scented, richly colored American hybrid. Flowers in late spring/early summer.

H: short; **F**: medium
◊ ◊ ☀ intermediate

Miltoniopsis **Grune de Becquet**
Stunning hybrid from the Eric Young Foundation in Jersey, Channel Islands, UK; produces huge, almost flat, award-quality flowers.

H: short; **F**: large
◊ ◊ ☀ intermediate

Miltoniopsis Newton Falls

Miltoniopsis Jean Carlson

Miltoniopsis Andy Easton

Miltoniopsis Hajime Ono

Miltoniopsis Grune de Becquet 'Saint Mary's'

Odontoglossum

From the Greek *odontos*, meaning "tooth," and *glossa* meaning "tongue," *Odontoglossum* are now considered to be part of the genus *Oncidium*. Found in cloud forests of mountainous South America, this generally cool-growing group has long been highly prized. In the 19th century, vast sums of money changed hands for the most sought-after specimens, particularly of *Odm. crispum*. Plants should be grown in a sphagnum mix, which is never allowed to dry out completely. Water quality is important, and only use half-strength orchid fertilizer. Repot annually. *Odontoglossum* prefer day temperatures of 55–73°F (13–23°C), with nights not below 50°F (10°C).

Odontoglossum crispum
Epiphyte from Colombia. Variable in the wild from white to pale rose, with or without spotting. Line-bred to produce showy white and blush-white flowers on arching stems.

H: medium; **F**: medium
◊ ◊ ☼   cool

Odontoglossum **Sorel Point**
Hybrid registered by the Eric Young Foundation, Jersey, using *Odm. crispum*; one of many hybrids from this parent. Flower spikes will need some staking.

H: medium; **F**: medium
◊ ◊ ☼   cool

Odontoglossum **Violetta von Holm**
Popular German hybrid with long-lasting flowers on one or more stems. A proven houseplant; the majority of *Odontoglossum* are not as tolerant.

H: medium; **F**: medium
◊ ◊ ☼   cool/intermediate

Odontoglossum praestans
South American, from Colombia to Peru. Produces star-shaped flowers on long, branching spikes that require extra space and some staking.

H: medium; **F**: medium
◊ ◊ ☼   cool

Odontoglossum crispum

Odontoglossum Sorel Point

Odontoglossum Violetta von Holm

Odontoglossum praestans

Odontoglossum alliance

The popularity of *Odontoglossum* gave rise to thousands of hybrids, which were difficult to grow. In an attempt to produce more tolerant plants, nurserymen used other genera, most commonly *Cochlioda, Miltonia,* and *Oncidium*, with *Odontoglossum* to create new, easier-to-grow hybrids. Most can be grown in a sphagnum moss mix or an open, peat-based orchid medium.

Odontioda **McBean's Eliza**
Bred from the Charlesworth *Odontoglossum* with *Cochlioda*. Prefers day temperatures of 59–79°F (15–26°C), with nights not below 54°F (12°C). Flower color varies from the palest lemon to strong yellow, with varying amounts of spotting.

H: medium; **F**: medium
◊ ◊ ☼ cool

Odontioda **McBean's Giselle**
Bred for strong patterning and color combinations on round flowers that are produced in late winter/early spring.

H: medium; **F**: medium
◊ ◊ ☼ cool

Odontocidium **Wildcat**
Very tolerant hybrid and proven houseplant that prefers intermediate temperatures and moderate humidity. Unhappy in a dry atmosphere. Produces long flower stems with many blooms. Can reflower within the year when grown well.

H: tall; **F**: medium
◊ ◊ ☼ intermediate

Rossioglossum grande
Known as the "clown orchid"; one of six species in this genus and native to the wet cloud forests of Mexico and Honduras. Each spike carries two to eight large, showy flowers.

H: medium; **F**: large
◊ ◊ ☼ intermediate

Odontioda McBean's Eliza   *Odontioda* McBean's Giselle

Odontocidium Wildcat

Rossioglossum grande

Odontoglossum alliance *continued*

Odontioda **McBean's Rosie**
Bred for red patterning on round flowers. A compact plant that flowers in late winter/early spring.

H: medium; **F**: medium
◊ ◊ ☼ cool/intermediate

Odontonia **Yellow Parade**
Pretty hybrid that prefers intermediate temperatures with moderate humidity. Produces eight or more blooms on a spike.

H: medium; **F**: medium
◊ ◊ ☼ intermediate

Odontioda **Florence Stirling**
Can be grown in cool to intermediate conditions; usually blooms in late winter. The flower spike will need to be staked. Flower patterns vary, since most plants are seed-raised. Very few on offer will be divisions, although occasionally a plant will grow large enough to be divided. The divisions will all flower in the same way.

H: medium; **F**: medium
◊ ◊ ☼ cool/intermediate

Odontocidium **Purbeck Gold**
Reliable houseplant hybrid, with *Onc. tigrinum* as one of its parents. Produces arching spikes of 10 or more flowers in the fall. Will require some staking. Grows best in intermediate conditions with good indirect light and high humidity. Reduce frequency of watering when temperatures fall, and increase light levels.

H: medium; **F**: medium
◊ ◊ ☼ intermediate

Odontioda McBean's Rosie

Odontonia Yellow Parade

Odontioda Florence Stirling

Odontocidium Purbeck Gold

Oncidium

A large genus, found in subtropical and tropical America. Most *Oncidium* are epiphytic and can be grown in intermediate conditions in free-draining, medium-grade orchid potting medium or bark, with frequent watering. Repot every other year in the spring, but not when the plant is in flower.

Oncidium Gower Ramsey

A proven houseplant. Tolerates high temperatures, combined with high humidity and good air movement. It can be grown in the home in intermediate conditions with moderate humidity. Produces slender branching sprays of flowers.

H: medium; **F**: medium
◊ ◊ ☼   intermediate/warm

Oncidium Sweet Sugar

A popular American hybrid and proven potted plant. Produces slender branching sprays of long-lasting flowers. Prefers day temperatures of 72–77°F (22–25°C), with nights around 55°F (13°C). Tolerates higher temperatures, as long as humidity and air movement are increased.

H: medium; **F**: medium
◊ ◊ ☼   intermediate/warm

Oncidium ornithorhynchum

Species found from Mexico to Colombia. Produces masses of small, fragrant flowers in white, pink, or lilac, on arching stems.

H: medium; **F**: small
◊ ◊ ☼   cool

Oncidium Twinkle

American hybrid, producing many spikes of small, fragrant, long-lasting cream or red flowers in winter. Prefers day temperatures of 81°F (27°C), with nights not below 55°F (13°C). Repot in alternate years, after flowering, into a small pot of fine-grade orchid medium or bark.

H: short; **F**: small
◊ ◊ ☼   intermediate

Oncidium Gower Ramsey

Oncidium Sweet Sugar

...idium ornithorhynchum

Oncidium Twinkle

Oncidium continued

Oncidium sphacelatum
Found from Mexico to Costa Rica and
Venezuela. Requires careful placement;
becomes a large plant with 3¼ ft- (1 m-)
long leaves and branching flower spikes
of up to 6½ ft (2 m). These can be
controlled with staking.

H: tall; **F**: small
◊ ◊ ☼ intermediate/warm

Oncidium tigrinum
Of Mexican origin. Brown barring on
the sepals and petals contrasts with the
large, bright yellow lip. Produces long
flower spikes that need some staking.

H: medium; **F**: medium
◊ ◊ ☼ intermediate

Oncidium **Sharry Baby**
American hybrid and proven houseplant.
Produces spikes of long-lasting,
chocolate-scented flowers. Can tolerate
higher temperatures as long as humidity
and air movement are increased. In a dry
atmosphere, a moist pebble tray will
help (*see pp. 34–35*).

H: medium; **F**: medium
◊ ◊ ☼ intermediate

Oncidium sphacelatum

Oncidium tigrinum

Oncidium Sharry Baby

Paphiopedilum (cool)

Known as the lady's slipper, Venus's slipper, or slipper orchid, this genus is found from southern India to New Guinea and the Philippines. Most have a single, glossy flower on each stem; cool-growing types are distinguished by their plain green leaves. A complex *Paphiopedilum* is a hybrid that contains several species or subspecies; the object has been to produce larger and rounder flowers. *Paphiopedilum* grows best in daytime temperatures around 57–64°F (14–18°C), with nights not below 50°F (10°C). Keep the medium moist but not wet, and use orchid fertilizer at half strength. Repot annually between March and June, when not in flower, using a bark and sphagnum mix. Large clumps can be divided (*see pp. 44–45*).

Paphiopedilum **Freckles**
Well-known American hybrid that produces a single flower on each stem in early winter. May be grown a little warmer than most complex *Paph*. Has been widely used for hybridizing.

H: short; **F**: large
◊ ◊ ☼ cool

Paphiopedilum insigne
Vigorous-growing plant from Nepal and northeast India. Usually produces a single flower on each stem. Can tolerate night temperatures down to 45°F (7°C).

H: short; **F**: medium
◊ ◊ ☼ cool

Paphiopedilum fairrieanum
Native of Nepal, Bhutan, and Sikkim, India. Produces single flowers, distinguished by their swept-back petals and slim leaves.

H: short; **F**: medium
◊ ◊ ☼ cool

Paphiopedilum Freckles

Paphiopedilum insigne

Paphiopedilum fairrieanum

Paphiopedilum (intermediate/warm)

The warmer-growing *Paphiopedilum* usually have mottled leaves or are classed as "multi-floral," with several blooms on each stem. Grow at day temperatures of 70–82°F (21–28°C), with nights not below 64°F (18°C). The higher the temperature, the higher the humidity needed. Keep the potting medium moist but not wet, and use orchid fertilizer at half strength. Using a bark and sphagnum moss mix, repot annually between March and June, when not in flower. Large clumps can be divided (*see pp. 44–45*).

Paphiopedilum rothschildianum
Much sought after, handsome species from north Borneo. Requires careful positioning, since it makes a sizeable plant. Produces spikes up to 18 in (45 cm) tall, each carrying one or two large flowers.

H: tall; **F**: large
◊ ◊ ☼ intermediate

Paphiopedilum **Saint Swithin**
Classic American multi-floral hybrid of 1901. Remains popular today for its striking striped dorsal sepal and long petals.

H: tall; **F**: large
◊ ◊ ☼ intermediate/warm

Paphiopedilum **Clair de Lune**
Handsome hybrid, registered by renowned orchid breeder Frederick Sander; slow-growing, with marbled foliage. Produces a single lime-green and white flower on each stem. Like many *Paph.* Maudiae hybrids, it is often used in floristry.

H: medium; **F**: large
◊ ◊ ☼ intermediate/warm

Paphiopedilum **Mount Toro**
American multi-floral hybrid. Produces four or more flowers with long twisted petals on each spike. Will require staking to show off the blooms.

H: tall; **F**: large
◊ ◊ ☼ intermediate/warm

Paphiopedilum rothschildianum

Paphiopedilum Saint Swithin

Paphiopedilum Clair de Lune

Paphiopedilum Mount Toro 'Watling Hall'

Phalaenopsis

This naturally epiphytic genus is the most popular orchid houseplant. It can produce flower spikes in any season and usually reflowers within the year (*see pp. 36–37*). *Phalaenopsis* grows best in indirect sun, with daytime temperatures above 68°F (20°C) and nights not below 60°F (16°C). Water thoroughly when the potting medium is almost dry and allow to drain; keep the center of the plant dry. The higher the temperature, the higher the humidity required, so in a dry atmosphere use a pebble tray (*see pp. 34–35*). Mist the leaves in the morning if the air is dry, and fertilize regularly (*see p. 33*). Repot every other year between March and June, but not when in flower.

Phalaenopsis Brother Pico Sweetheart "K&P"
Popular Taiwanese, cloned hybrid. Compact plant with many small, long-lasting flowers; likes good humidity.

H: medium; **F**: small
◊ ◊ ☼ warm

Phalaenopsis violacea
Short plant with large, apple-green leaves. Produces two or three fragrant flowers, usually in late summer. Color can vary.

H: short; **F**: medium
◊ ◊ ☼ warm

Phalaenopsis Brother Little Amaglad
Taiwanese hybrid, producing small but long-lasting flowers. A proven houseplant.

H: medium; **F**: small
◊ ◊ ☼ warm

Phalaenopsis I-Hsin Black Tulip
Modern Taiwanese hybrid with deep, red-wine coloring. Patterning may vary.

H: medium; **F**: medium
◊ ◊ ☼ warm

Phalaenopsis equestris
Small and delicate with branching multi-floral spikes. Grow slightly drier.

H: short; **F**: small
◊ ☼ warm

Phalaenopsis Brother Pico Sweetheart 'K&P'

Phalaenopsis violacea

alaenopsis Brother Little Amaglad   *Phalaenopsis* I-Hsin Black Tulip   *Phalaenopsis equestris*

Phragmipedium

Found in Central and South America, *Phragmipedium* is another genus of slipper orchid. It grows best in daytime temperatures around 68°F (20°C), with nights not below 60°F (16°C), in an airy spot with indirect light. The higher the temperature, the higher the humidity needed, so in a dry atmosphere use a pebble tray (*see pp. 34–35*). Plants require a sphagnum moss mix or a medium orchid mix containing peat, and copious watering when in growth. Never allow the medium to dry out completely at any time of the year, but do not let the pot sit in water. Repot each year in spring when out of flower. *Phragmipedium* prefers to grow in large clumps rather than being divided frequently.

Phragmipedium Olaf Gruss
German hybrid, in shades of pink. Displays characteristics from both of its parents, *Phrag. besseae* and *Phrag. pearcei*.

H: medium; **F**: medium
◊ ◊ ☼ intermediate

Phragmipedium schlimii
Originates in Colombia. Forms dense clumps up to 20 in (50 cm) in height, but usually shorter when in cultivation. The attractive flowers are small for the genus but very distinctive.

H: medium; **F**: medium
◊ ◊ ☼ intermediate

Phragmipedium besseae
Found on the eastern slopes of the Andes. Produces up to four spectacular flowers on stems that can be quite tall, and sometimes branched.

H: medium; **F**: medium
◊ ◊ ☼ intermediate

Phragmipedium China Dragon
American hybrid, bred to bring the coloring of *Phrag. besseae* to the large flowers of *Phrag. grande*. Grow in a heated greenhouse rather than in the home.

H: medium; **F**: large
◊ ◊ ☼ intermediate

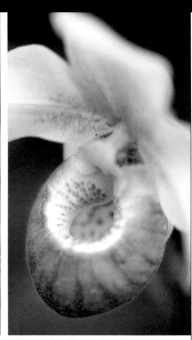

Phragmipedium Olaf Gruss

Phragmipedium schlimii

Phragmipedium besseae

Phragmipedium China Dragon

Pleione

Known as the "Indian crocus" and found from India to Taiwan and Thailand, *Pleione* is a genus of small, attractive, deciduous plants with relatively large flowers. Requiring minimal winter protection, it can be grown in a cold frame if nighttime temperatures are just above freezing; it likes a small pot and a very free-draining potting medium of sphagnum moss, fine bark, and perlite. Leave about one-third of the pseudobulb showing above the top of the medium; space pseudobulbs about ¾ in (2 cm) apart. Water sparingly when in flower, keeping the medium just damp, then water freely while the leaves and roots are growing. Reduce watering as the leaves yellow, and give plants a complete rest when the leaves brown and drop off; allow a cool rest period over winter.

Pleione formosana
Prefers frost-free winter nights of 34–41°F (1–5°C) and summer daytime temperatures below 77°F (25°C). Can be in a north-facing window when in growth.

H: short; **F**: large
◊ ◊ R ☼ cool

Pleione **Britannia 'Doreen'**
A choice clone of this well-known hybrid. Noted for its larger flowers and broader lip. Produces long-lasting blooms in early spring.

H: short; **F**: large
◊ ◊ R ☼ cool

Pleione **Shantung**
Sought-after hybrid; strong grower. Produces large blooms in early spring, in yellow to apricot with spotted, frilly lips.

H: short; **F**: large
◊ ◊ R ☼ cool

Pleione forrestii
The only *Pleione* species to have yellow flowers; used extensively in the breeding of yellow hybrids. Found on mossy rocks in China and northern Myanmar.

H: short; **F**: large
◊ ◊ R ☼ cool

Pleione formosana

Pleione Britannia 'Doreen'

ione Shantung 'Ducat'

Pleione forrestii

Prosthechea

Consisting mainly of epiphytes, this group occurs in Florida, Mexico, and tropical America. Recently reestablished as a genus. *Prosthechea* includes several species formerly included in *Encyclia*.

Prosthechea mariae

Slightly pendulous species from northeast Mexico. Grow on a raft suspended in a cool place with good light. When in growth, plunge plants into water daily or spray heavily. Stop watering when growth is complete, and lower temperatures to around 36–41°F (2–5°C). In spring, spray roots and raise the temperature to encourage growth.

H: medium; **F**: large
dd R ☼ cool

Prosthechea radiata

Grows in various forest types in Guatemala, Honduras, and Mexico. A compact plant with fragrant flowers. Easy to grow in a basket in a coarse bark mix, or mounted on a raft.

H: short/medium; **F**: medium
◊ ◊ ☼ cool/intermediate

Prosthechea vitellina

Produces stunning, long-lasting blooms in spring or fall. Leaves have a blue-gray bloom. Grows best in good humidity, with day temperatures above 68°F (20°C), in a sphagnum moss mix. Prefers a uniform regime all year round.

H: short; **F**: medium
◊ ◊ ☼ warm

Prosthechea cochleata

Can become a sizeable, though not tall, plant. Each stem carries several blooms that open successively for a long flowering period; mature plants can flower all year round. Grows best in daytime temperatures above 68°F (20°C), with nights not below 60°F (16°C). Repot every other year between March and June, when not in flower.

H: short/medium; **F**: medium
◊ ☼ intermediate

Prosthechea mariae 'Herrenhausen'   *Prosthechea radiata*

Prosthechea vitellina

Prosthechea cochleata

Vanda

These showy epiphytes are not easy to keep in the home, but can be grown with or without a coarse bark medium in slatted baskets, or suspended from a wire to accommodate their trailing roots. Bright sunlight is ideal. Drench daily to keep humidity high, and use dilute foliar feed when in growth. Most hybrids need a minimum winter night temperature of 60°F (16°C), and flower in fall or winter. Any fluctuation in conditions may cause the plant to shed its lower leaves. Removing the lower portion of the stem, keeping the healthy younger roots, will help maintain vigor. Care should be taken when watering: follow instructions, and never let the roots sit in water. *Vanda* is often sold in tall glass vases (*see p. 14*).

Vanda **Saphir**

Hybrid registered by horticulturalist James Veitch, with vibrant lavender-blue flowers.

H: tall; **F**: large
◊ ◊ ☼ warm

Vanda *coerulea*

The most famous *Vanda*; an endangered species that has been produced commercially from seed to protect the remaining wild population. Grown cooler than other species in this group, with a winter night minimum of 54°F (12°C).

H: short; **F**: large
◊ ◊ ☼ warm

Euanthe *sanderiana*

Commonly but incorrectly known as *Vanda sanderiana*; Sander himself refused to accept the classification. Prefers light, humid conditions, shaded from midday sun. Water well, reducing frequency when temperatures fall.

H: tall; **F**: large
◊ ◊ ☼ warm

Vanda **Noranga's Top Notch**

Modern Australian hybrid that produces large, round flowers.

H: tall; **F**: large
◊ ◊ ☼ warm

Vanda Saphir   Vanda coerulea

Euanthe sanderiana

Vanda Noranga's Top Notch

Zygopetalum and intergenerics

The species is found in South and Central America, the majority in the higher elevations of Brazil. Although tolerant, *Zygopetalum* grows best in temperatures around 63–77°F (17–25°C), with nights not below 55°F (13°C). It can tolerate greatly varying temperatures, up to 95°F (35°C), and provided day temperatures are warmer, can survive brief spells with night temperatures just above freezing. It prefers indirect sunlight and moderate humidity. Grow in sphagnum moss mixed with perlite and bark, repotting every year. Water freely when in growth, and less frequently in the winter, never letting the sphagnum dry out. Use a balanced orchid fertilizer during the summer, and one with increased potash from fall to late spring.

Zygoneria **Adelaide Meadows**
An Australian hybrid bred from a *Neogardeneria*. Most sold are from seed, causing some variation, but are usually compact plants with fragrant flowers.

H: medium; **F**: medium
◊ ◊ ☼ intermediate

Zygopetalum maculatum
Produces fragrant, showy flowers. Can be left to grow into a sizeable plant, or divided, when large enough, into pieces with at least three pseudobulbs each.

H: medium; **F**: medium
◊ ◊ ☼ intermediate

Zygopetalum **Centenary**
Large, round flowers with solid coloring are the norm for this Australian hybrid. Has produced several award-winning plants.

H: medium; **F**: medium
◊ ◊ ☼ intermediate

Zygopetalum **Titanic**
Australian hybrid and proven houseplant. When mature, will produce several spikes of fragrant blooms in spring/early summer. It sometimes reflowers within the year.

H: medium; **F**: medium
◊ ◊ ☼ intermediate

Zygoneria Adelaide Meadows   *Zygopetalum maculatum*

Zygopetalum Centenary

Zygopetalum Titanic

Intergenerics

The commercial hybridizer aims to produce new orchids that are eye-catching, easy to grow, and have long-lasting blooms. As a result, an increasing number of orchids have been produced using one or more closely related genera. These man-made "intergeneric" hybrids require new genus names, which often leads to confusion. However, successful high-quality plants will then be mericloned (*see pp. 136-137*) and made available to the general public.

Beallara **Peggy Ruth Carpenter**

Results from crossing plants within *Brassia*, *Cochlioda*, *Miltonia*, *Odontoglossum*, and *Oncidium*. A favorite and a proven houseplant. Each spike carries four or more blooms. It can become a large plant.

H: medium; **F**: large
◊ ☼ intermediate/warm

Bakerara **Samurai**

Results from crossing plants within *Brassia*, *Miltonia*, and *Odontoglossum*. Slow growing and compact, it prefers medium/good humidity.

H: medium; **F**: medium
◊ ☼ intermediate

Burrageara **Nelly Isler**

Results from crossing plants within *Cochlioda*, *Miltonia*, *Odontoglossum*, and *Oncidium*. A proven potted plant, with two or more stems of fragrant, long-lasting flowers. Grows best in daytime temperatures of 66–77°F (19–25°C), with nights not below 57°F (14°C).

H: medium; **F**: medium
◊ ☼ intermediate/warm

Colmanara **Masai**

Results from crossing plants within *Miltonia*, *Odontoglossum*, and *Oncidium*. Produces upright spikes of seven or more flowers. Grow as for *Bakerara*.

H: medium; **F**: medium
◊ ☼ intermediate

Beallara Peggy Ruth Carpenter

Bakerara Samurai

Burrageara Nelly Isler

Colmanara Masai 'Splash'

Troubleshooting

Provided you have chosen the right orchid to suit the conditions you can provide, growing one in the home can be as easy as growing any other houseplant. Orchids are generally trouble-free, in spite of the mystique surrounding them, and most concerns have simple solutions.

How can I encourage my moth orchid to reflower?

Check that it is warm enough. If conditions are satisfactory and you have followed the advice on pages 36–37, try reducing the temperature by 9°F (5°C) for four weeks.

Why are there sticky droplets on the stem of my orchid?

These are beads of sap—possibly a sign that the plant is stressed. Check growing conditions (*refer to the directory on pp. 72–133*), and watch out for ants, which can be attracted by the sweet-tasting sap.

Can potted houseplant orchids be left without water when I'm on vacation?

For up to two weeks, your orchid should be fine. Water thoroughly and drain, then leave in a shady position. A month's vacation would require a friend to check on the plants after two weeks. Warn them – if in doubt, don't water it.

Should orchids be put outside in the summer?

This depends on your climate and the orchid. Generally, orchids sold as houseplants should be kept indoors.

Can *Cymbidium* leaves be cut back for a neater appearance?

The leaves are needed to make food for the plant and will not regrow if cut.

Can aerial roots be removed to improve the look of an orchid?

Aerial roots are needed to absorb moisture from the atmosphere. However, if they are dried-out and dead, they are of no use to the orchid and can be neatly removed. If this happens, check humidity levels and consider using a pebble tray (*see pp. 34–35*).

Bud drop

This problem is most commonly caused by a shock, such as a sudden change of temperature. This could occur as a result of poor wrapping after purchase, or by abruptly moving the plant from a cool spot to a much warmer one. A draft or a particularly dry atmosphere can also cause stress to your orchid, so do take care when positioning it (*see pp. 28–29*). If a dry atmosphere is the likely cause, increase humidity by using a pebble tray (*see pp. 34–35*). With the necessary adjustments to the growing conditions, the plant should flower successfully the next time around.

Frost damage

Exposing *Cymbidium* to frost in a greenhouse will kill most, if not all of the growth, turning it brown. *Cymbidium* are tough plants, however, and a single green shoot will often appear, which can be removed with a back bulb attached and planted (*see pp. 46–47*).

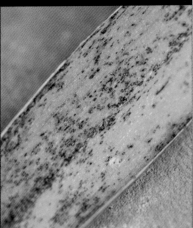

Mealy bug

These insects suck sap, weakening plants, and can spread viruses. They hide in crevices: where the leaves meet the stem, at the base of the plant, and even on flowers. They can be eradicated with a suitable insecticide, or with the biological control *Cryptolaemus montrouzieri*.

Slug damage

Snails and slugs can eat their way through flower buds and fleshy leaves, and can accidentally be carried indoors when bringing an orchid in from outside. Their presence is marked by their slimy trail. Either pick the pests off individually or use suitable pellets, if appropriate.

Red spider mite

A relatively rare pest on orchids, and difficult to spot until damage has been caused. Holes appear in both leaves and flowers, and leaf surfaces have a silvery-gray appearance. Existing pesticides are not suitable for use on orchids, so use the biological control, *Phytoseiulus persimilis*.

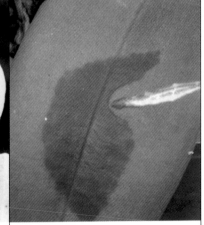

Scale

Soft-shelled brown scale and a hard-shelled gray scale can sometimes attack stems or leaves. Picking them off by hand is time-consuming; you can spray plants with an appropriate insecticide, but do check current recommendations before doing so.

Gray mold

Also known as *Botrytis*, this fungal disease is a sign of poor growing conditions; leading to small black spots on the flower petals. Poor air circulation is the usual cause. Remove affected flowers, and improve growing conditions and airflow (*see pp. 72–133*) to prevent the disease reoccurring.

Leaf damage

An unsightly condition, mostly caused by exposure to direct light through a window; the sun's rays fall directly on to the leaf, destroying cells. There is no cure for the damaged leaf. Move the plant out of direct sunlight, and, with great care, remove the leaf with a sharp, sterile blade.

Glossary

Growing orchids involves many specific botanical and technical terms.
This glossary explains these, and will give you a better understanding
of growing orchids.

A

Acid With a pH value below 7.
Aerial root A root growing above the ground that absorbs moisture.
Alkaline With a pH value above 7.
Alliance A group of similar genera.

B

Back bulb An old, dormant pseudobulb (*see Pseudobulb*).
Biological control The use of predatory organisms to eradicate pests.

C

Calcareous Composed of, containing, or characteristic of calcium carbonate, calcium, or limestone.
Capsule Pod that contains the seed.
Clone Genetically identical to its parent and siblings.
Column The fused style and stamens.
Compost Decayed kitchen scraps and yard waste used as a natural fertilizer.
Cross Offspring, a new plant resulting from cross-pollination.
Crown The heart of the plant where the leaves converge.

D

Deciduous A plant that loses its leaves and dies down annually at the end of the growing season.

Differential Relating to, or showing, a difference.
Distilled water Pure water; made by boiling tap water and condensing the steam. It can also be bought.
Divisions Sections of plant resulting from propagating a plant by division.
Dolomite lime Powdered lime, used to neutralize acidic soil/potting medium.
Dormant Not actively growing.
Dorsal sepal Sepal opposite the lip, usually uppermost in the flower.

E

Epiphyte Grows on another plant for support but is not parasitic.
Floriferous Bears flowers freely.

F

Fungicide A chemical treatment used to control fungal diseases.

G

Genus Closely related group of species.
Gross feeders Plants that require a lot of nutrients to maintain their health.

H

Habit Natural tendency or growth form.
Habitat Ecological or environmental area inhabited by a particular plant.

Humidity The moisture content of the air; all orchids like humid conditions.
Humus Decomposed organic matter found in the soil, usually nearer the surface.
Hybrid Plant with genetically distinct parents.
Hybridizing The controlled interbreeding of two known parent plants.

I

Insecticide A treatment specifically used to control insect pests.
Intergeneric A hybrid made up of two or more genera.

K

Keiki Small plantlet that develops on the stem. Can be used in propagation.

L

Labellum Lip, the third petal of an orchid flower; the lowest.
Lateral sepal Sepal either side of the lip, held below the petals.
Lead The growing point of a plant.
Leaf litter The natural accumulation of fallen leaves on the soil surface.
Leaf mold Composted leaf matter, often naturally found beneath leaf litter; it can be made by composting leaves.

Lip A modified third petal (*see labellum*).
Lithophyte Grows on rocks in their natural habitat.
Loam Fertile, well-drained, moisture-retentive soil, usually containing equal parts sand, clay, and silt.

M

Medium Planting matter.
Mericlone Cloned plant produced in the laboratory from plant tissue.
Micropropagation The propagation of plants in sterile laboratory conditions, often in large numbers.
Monopodial Growing as a single stem or rhizome.
Multi-floral The flower spike holds more than one bloom.
Mycorrhiza Fungal mycelium needed to be present for orchid seeds to germinate successfully.

N

Naturalized A plant totally established in a habitat following introduction.
Node Point of stem from which a leaf or growth bud emerges.
Nomenclature A set or system of names and naming.

P

Peat substitute Organic matter, such as composted bark, used as a green alternative to peat.
Perlite Beads of pumice stone.
Pesticide A treatment used to control pests, including insects.
Petals Inner whorl of flower parts.
Pheromones Chemical signals that trigger a natural response.
Plantlet Small plant or keiki.
Pod Capsule that contains the seed.
Pollination The transfer of pollen to the stigma.
Pollinia The massed pollen grains within the flower.
Pseudobulb Thickened bulblike section of stem that stores water and nutrients.

R

Raft A flat piece of cork or bark for mounting epiphytes.
Rhizome Specialized stem growing on or below the surface, producing roots and shoots along its length.
Rockwool Spun basaltic rock.
Root-bound When the plant roots have overfilled and outgrown the capacity of the container.
Rosette Leaves radiating from a common center.

S

Sepals Outer whorl of flower parts.
Sequential flowering Opening of flower buds over a period of time.

Sphagnum moss Spongy moss that grows on peat bogs.
Species Basic member of a genus; each one genetically similar.
Spike Flower stem and head.
Spur Tubelike extension at the back of the lip of some orchids.
Stamen The male floral organ.
Stigma The female floral organ that receives pollen.
Stigmatic surface The area of the flower, usually sticky, beneath the anther cap that receives pollen.
Sympodial Where new growth arises from the rhizome of a previous growth.

T

Temperate zones The geographical zones that lie between the tropics and arctic circles.
Terrestrial Grows in or on the soil or surface litter.
Tuber Swollen stem, branch, or root.

V

Variety Natural variation in a species.

Suppliers and additional resources

Many of these suppliers are specialized nurseries, so it is worth checking for opening hours before visiting, especially if you are making a long trip.

US suppliers

Carter and Holmes Orchids, Inc.
P.O. Box 668
629 Mendenhall Road
Newberry, SC
29108
800-873-7086
www.carterandholmes.com
This third-generation orchid specialist offers a wide selection at reasonable prices, and works with Orchids in Our Tropics in Canada for wider distribution.

Orchids by Hausermann
2N134 Addison Road
Villa Park, IL
60181-1191
630-543-6855
www.orchidsbyhausermann.com
orchidorders@orchidsbyhausermann.com
This large Midwestern grower has been in business since 1935, and offers a wide variety, but specializes in Cattleya types.

Parkside Orchids
2503 Mountainview Drive
Ottsville, PA
18942
610-847-8039
www.parksideorchids.com
This orchid nursery has a wide selection, and their website shows plants available in bud.

R. F. Orchids
28100 SW 182nd Avenue
Homestead, FL
33030
305-245-4570
Order line: 877-967-1284
www.rforchids.com
This nursery specializes in Vanda, Asconcendra, and their relatives, including dwarf cultivars.

Santa Barbara Orchid Estate
1250 Orchid Drive
Santa Barbara, CA
93111
805-967-1284
www.sborchid.com
A great variety of orchids on offer; specialists in outdoor orchids.

Canadian suppliers

Orchids in Our Tropics
15 Wilmac Court
Gormley, Ontario
Canada
L0H 1G0
905-727-3319
www.orchidsinourtropics.com
See Carter and Holmes Orchids, Inc. for information.

Paramount Orchids
1060-101 Street SW
Calgary, Alberta
Canada
T3H 3Z5
403-686-7021
www.paramountorchids.com
This Canadian source specializes in intermediate- to warm-growing orchids, and will ship to the US with a minimum order of $75 (Canadian).

Orchid societies

The American Orchid Society
16700 AOS Lane
Delray Beach, FL
33446
561-404-2000
www.aos.org
Membership includes the full-color magazine Orchid, a bookstore, lists of suppliers, events, booklets, discussion forums, and more.

International Phalaenopsis Alliance
1540 Anne Drive
West Chester, PA
19380
610-431-7633
www.phal.org
Members receive a full-color magazine devoted to Phalaenopsis, and details on national and local orchid workshops.

Orchid Digest
P.O. Box 10360
Canoga Park, CA
91309
membership@orchiddigest.org
www.orchiddigest.org
Members receive the monthly full-color magazine Orchid Digest.

Canadian Orchid Congress
www.canadianorchidcongress.ca
This association of more than 20 Canadian orchid societies is dedicated to serving orchid growers and hobbyists through shows, publications, lectures, and seminars.

Orchid Society of Great Britain
103 North Road
Three Bridges
Crawley
West Sussex, UK
RH10 1SQ
+44 1293 528615
www.orchid-society-gb.org.uk

Orchid shows

Miami International Orchid Show
305-255-3656
www.southfloridaorchidsociety.org.
Sponsored by the South Florida Orchid
Society, usually held in February, in
Miami, Florida. Contact the Society
for the next location and time.

New York Botanical Garden
Orchid Show
200th Street and Kazimiroff Blvd.
The Bronx, NY
10460
639-967-5268
www.nybg.org
Sponsored by the New York Orchid
Society and usually held in March or
April at Rockefeller Center. For
information, visit the website above.

Pacific Orchid Exposition
San Francisco Orchid Society
P.O. Box 27145
San Francisco, CA
94127
425-665-2468
www.orchidsanfrancisco.org
One of the three major orchid shows in
North America. Visit the website for
details of upcoming shows.

Santa Barbara International
Orchid Show
231 Middle Road
Santa Barbara, CA
93108-2449
805-969-5746
www.sborchidshow.com
One of North America's major orchid
shows. Visit the website for dates.

Where to see orchids

Atlanta Botanical Garden
1345 Piedmont Avenue
Atlanta, GA
30309
404-867-5859
www.atlantabotanicalgarden.org
State-of-the-art Fuqua Orchid Center,
research library, and events.

Brooklyn Botanic Garden
1000 Washington Avenue
Brooklyn, NY
11225
718-622-4433
www.bbg.org

Longwood Gardens
106 State Street
Kennet Square, PA
19348
610-388-1000
www.longwoodgardens.org

Missouri Botanic Gardens
4344 Shaw Avenue
St. Louis, MO
63110
314-577-5100
www.mobot.org
World-class orchid collection and display.

New York Botanical Garden
The Bronx, NY
639-967-5268
www.nybg.org

Further reading

Orchids (American Orchid Society).
Subscription free as part of the
membership package.

Journal of the International
Phalaenopsis Alliance. For
information on joining, see the entry
on the previous page.

Canadian Orchid Congress
newsletter. For online newsletter, visit
the organization's website.

Index

Index

Acknowledgments

The publisher would like to thank the following for their kind permission to reproduce their photographs:

(Key: a-above; b-below/bottom; c-center; l-left; r-right; t-top)

8 Garden World Images: A. Graham. **9** Alamy Images: The Natural History Museum (tc) (tr); Corbis: Lindsay Hebberd (c); David Ridgeway (br). **11** Photolibrary: Brigitte Merle (tr). **12** Liz Johnson (bl); Alamy Images: Mike Booth (br); Wildlife GmbH (t). **13** David Ridgeway (tr); Liz Johnson (c) (bl); **14** Alamy Images: CuboImages srl. **15** Alamy Images: Rob Walls (bl). **16-17** Science Photo Library: Adrian Bicker. **17** Alamy Images: fotoFlora (bl); Maximilian Weinzierl (t). Eric Hunt: (c). Natural Visions: Colin Paterson-Jones (br). **18** GAP Photos: John Glover. **19** Alamy Images: aaron peterson.net (br). Dr. Henry Oakeley: (t). Harpur Garden Library: Jerry Harpur (bl). **23** Alamy Images: Maximilian Weinzierl (cl). GAP Photos: Jenny Lilly (tr). naturepl.com: Vivek Menon (bl). **25** Alamy Images: Nigel Cattlin (br). **27** Garden World Images: John Swithinbank (t). **28** GAP Photos: Friedrich Strauss (t) (bl) Liz Johnson (br). **29** Corbis: Philip Harvey (tl). Photolibrary: Lynne Brotchie (tr). **33** Garden World Images: MAP/N & P Mioulane (br). **42** Photoshot: Photos Horticultural. **47** Marilyn Hunt: (tr). **62** GAP Photos: J S Sira. **63** Corbis: Dennis Johnson, Papilio (br). Garden World Images: Gilles Delacroix (cl). Getty Images: Kate Mathis (tr). **64** Liz Johnson (b); Alamy Images: Imagebroker (t). **65** Alamy Images: Imagebroker (r). Corbis: Mike Grandmaison (tl). Garden World Images:

MAP/N & P Mioulane (bl). **66** Corbis: Bryan Knox, Papilio (b). GAP Photos: Tim Gainey (t). **67** Alamy Images: Bob Gibbons (r); Nick Greaves (bl). Corbis: Steve & Ann Toon/Robert Harding World Imagery (tl). **68** Alamy Images: Hideo Kurihara (b). **68-69** Photolibrary: Chris Burrows. **69** Alamy Images: Arco Images GmbH (br); Susanne Masters (bl). **70** Alamy Images: Dave & Sigrun Tollerton (t). Photoshot: NHPA (b). **71** Alamy Images: Holmes Garden Photos (bc). Corbis: Tony Wharton, Frank Lane Picture Agency (r). **74** Dr. Henry Oakeley: (tr). Photoshot: Photos Horticultural (tl). **75** Garden World Images: MAP/A Descat/Collection Vacherot-Lecoufle. **76** Alamy Images: CuboImages srl (br). **78** Alamy Images: CuboImages srl (tl). **82** Liz Johnson. **83** Liz Johnson (t) Alamy Images: John Glover (bl). **84** Photoshot: Photos Horticultural (bc) (br). **86** Liz Johnson (tl) (cr) (b); Alamy Images: CuboImages (tr). **88** Liz Johnson (b) **90** Photoshot: Photos Horticultural (b). **92** Garden World Images: Sarah Lee (tl). Marilyn Hunt: (tr). **94** Alamy Images: blickwinkel (br). GAP Photos: Geoff Kidd (bc). **96** Alamy Images: blickwinkel (t). Eric Hunt: (b). **97** Alamy Images: John Glover. **98** Dr. Henry Oakeley: (br). Photolibrary: Howard Rice (bc). **102** Science Photo Library: Paul Harcourt-Davies (tc); Liz Johnson (tr). **103** Garden World Images: T Sims. **104** Liz Johnson (tl) (tr) (bl) (br). **106** Liz Johnson (t) (bl). **108** Liz Johnson (tl) (tr); Camera Press: Christoph Koester/Flora (b). **110** Liz Johnson (t) (bl); Garden World Images: (br). Marilyn Hunt: (bc). **111** Alamy Images: John Glover. **112** Garden World Images: T. Sims. **113** Alamy Images: Mike Booth (br). **114** Alamy Images: ArcoImages

GmbH (t). **116** Garden World Images: Eric Crichton (t); Liz Johnson (b). **118** Photolibrary: CuboImages. **121** GAP Photos: S & O (br). **122** Alamy Images: Glenn Harper (tr). Garden World Images: MAP/Arnaud Descat (b). **124** Alamy Images: Zena Elea (b). **125** Alamy Images: John Glover (bl). Garden World Images: Liz Cole (br). **126** Alamy Images: Mike Booth (b). Photoshot: Photos Horticultural (tr). **128** Alamy Images: Danita Delimont (b). Garden Exposures Photo Library: Andrea Jones (tr). **130** Liz Johnson (tl) (b); S & O Mathews Photography: (tr). **132** Alamy Images: Floralpik (t). **134** Liz Johnson (l)

All other images © Dorling Kindersley
For further information see:
www.dkimages.com

Dorling Kindersley would also like to thank:
Editorial assistance: Chauney Dunford and Becky Shackleton

Illustration: Carolyn Jenkins

Floral design: Jeanne Picot,
The Wild Orchid, Uckfield, East Sussex, England, +44 1825 733485
www.thewildorchid.co.uk

Index: Chris Bernstein

Location: The Rainbow Inn, Cooksbridge, East Sussex, England, +44 1273 400334, www.rainbowsussex.com

McBean's Orchids: Jim Durrant, Shelley Butler, Sarah Butler, and Andy Symonds

Photographer's assistant: Richard Horsly